Laboratory Practice

Nonclinical Laboratory Studies

Concise Reference

Good Laboratory Practice

Nonclinical Laboratory Studies

Concise Reference

Good Laboratory Practice: Nonclinical Laboratory Studies Concise Reference

Copyright © 2010 by PharmaLogika, Inc

PharmaLogika

PharmaLogika, Inc.
PO Box 461
Willow Springs, NC 27592

www.pharmalogika.com

Author / Editor. Mindy J. Allport-Settle

Published by PharmaLogika, Inc.

Printed in the United States of America. First Printing.

ISBN 0-9830719-1-8
ISBN-13 978-0-9830719-1-4

Contents

Part I

Federal Regulations Relating to Good Laboratory Practice 33

Part 58: Good Laboratory Practice for Nonclinical Laboratory Studies 35

Part II

Guidance Documents **111**

Bioresearch Monitoring Good Laboratory Practice **113**

Part III

Redbook 2000 179

Redbook 2000: IV.B.1 General Guidelines for Designing and Conducting Toxicity Studies 181

Preface

About this Book

This book is designed to be a unified reference source for the U.S. Food and Drug Adminstration's Good Laboratory Practice regulations, guidance, and associated documents for pharmaceutical, biologics and medical device products nonclinical trials.

The included *FDA Overview and Orientation* (Chapter 2 of this book) is designed to provide a foundation for understanding the background of the FDA, its guidelines, its relationship with other countries and its relationship with manufacturers and distributors.

This book is designed to be used both as a reference for experienced industry representatives and as a training resource for those new to the industry.

Included Documents and Features

Good Laboratory Practice Regulations and Guidance:

- *FDA Overview and Orientation*
- *Overview of GCP and Introduction to GLP*
- *Part I: Federal Regulations Relating to Good Laboratory Practice*
    - *Parts 58: Good Laboratory Practice for Nonclinical Laboratory Studies*
    - *1987 Final Rule - Good Laboratory Practice Regulations*
- *Part II: Guidance Documents*
    - *Bioresearch Monitoring Good Laboratory Practice*
    - *Good Laboratory Practices Questions and Answers*
- *Part III: Redbook 2000*
    - *IV.B.1 General Guidelines for Designing and Conducting Toxicity Studies*
    - *IV.B.2 Guidelines for Reporting the Results of Toxicity Studies*

Reference Tools

- *Part IV: Combined Glossary and Index*

About the Reference Tools

FDA Overview and Orientation and the Overview of GCP and Introduction to GLP

The FDA overview provides the reader with a brief history of the Food and Drug Administration (FDA) and explains not only what good clinical practice is, but why it exists and how it came to be. The overview of GCP provides the basic background for clinical trial management while the introduction to GLP provides a guide to the FDA's approach to nonclinical trial management.

Combined Glossary

The Combined Glossary includes all of the glossaries from each regulation and guidance listed alphabetically rather than by document.

When a word or term appears multiple times in the regulation and guidance documents, the word will appear multiple times in the Combined Glossary if there is a variation in the definition. Each duplicate entry is indented to highlight that it is a duplicate and the earliest reference to the entry is listed first. The source for each entry is bracketed (i.e., [21 CFR § 50]) for ease of reference. While the definitions are similar from one regulatory or guidance document to the next, they are not always identical.

Combined Index for all Regulations

The index is composed of a list of both words and terms specific to the Good Laboratory Practice regulations and includes selected entires relative to Good Clinical Practice.

Pharmaceutical, biotechnology, and medical device companies use terminology that combines scientific and technical jargon with legal phrases and concepts.

The index provides keywords and terminology as a tool to easily locate specific references across all documents rather than having to rely on memory or paging through each document individually.

FDA Overview and Orientation

The Food and Drug Administration (FDA)

The United States Food and Drug Administration (FDA) is responsible for protecting and promoting the nation's public health.

The programs for safety regulation vary widely by the type of product, its potential risks, and the regulatory powers granted to the agency. For example, the FDA regulates almost every facet of prescription drugs, including testing, manufacturing, labeling, advertising, marketing, efficacy and safety. FDA regulation of cosmetics, however, is focused primarily on labeling and safety. The FDA regulates most products with a set of published standards enforced by a combination of facility inspections, voluntary company reporting standards, and public and consumer watchdog activity.

The FDA frequently works in conjunction with other Federal agencies including the Department of Agriculture, Drug Enforcement Administration, Customs and Border Protection, and Consumer Product Safety Commission.

Historical Origins of Federal Food and Drug Regulation

Prior to the 20th century, there were few federal laws regulating the contents and sale of domestically produced food and pharmaceuticals before the 20th century (with one exception being the short-lived Vaccine Act of 1813). Some state laws provided varying degrees of protection against unethical sales practices, such as misrepresenting the ingredients of food products or therapeutic substances.

The history of the FDA can be traced to the latter part of the 19th century and the U.S. Department of Agriculture's Division of Chemistry (later Bureau of Chemistry). Under Harvey Washington Wiley, appointed chief chemist in 1883, the Division began conducting research into the adulteration and misbranding of food and drugs on the American market. Although they had no regulatory powers, the Division published its findings from 1887 to 1902 in a ten-part series entitled Foods and Food Adulterants. Wiley used these findings, and alliances with diverse organizations (such as state regulators, the

General Federation of Women's Clubs, and national associations of physicians and pharmacists) to lobby for a new federal law to set uniform standards for food and drugs to enter into interstate commerce.

Wiley's advocacy came at a time when the public had become alert to hazards in the marketplace by journalists and became part of a general trend for increased federal regulation in matters pertinent to public safety during the Progressive Era.[1] The 1902 Biologics Control Act was put in place after diphtheria antitoxin was collected from a horse named Jim who also had tetanus, resulting in several deaths.

The 1906 Food and Drug Act and creation of the FDA

In June 1906, President Theodore Roosevelt signed into law the Food and Drug Act, also known as the "Wiley Act" after its chief advocate.[2] The Act prohibited, under penalty of seizure of goods, the interstate transport of food which had been "adulterated," with that term referring to the addition of fillers of reduced "quality or strength," coloring to conceal "damage or inferiority," formulation with additives "injurious to health," or the use of "filthy, decomposed, or putrid" substances. The act applied similar penalties to the interstate marketing of "adulterated" drugs, in which the "standard of strength, quality, or purity" of the active ingredient was not either stated clearly on the label or listed in the United States Pharmacopoeia or the National Formulary. The act also banned "misbranding" of food and drugs.[3] The responsibility for examining food and drugs for such "adulteration" or "misbranding" was given to Wiley's USDA Bureau of Chemistry.[4] Strength, quality, identity, potency, and purity (SQuIPP) are currently the key product safety standards, with only two measures added since 1906 Act.

Wiley used these new regulatory powers to pursue an aggressive campaign against the manufacturers of foods with chemical additives, but the Chemistry Bureau's authority was soon checked by judicial decisions, as well as by the creation of the Board of Food and Drug Inspection and the Referee Board of Consulting Scientific Experts as separate organizations within the USDA in 1907 and 1908 respectively. A 1911 Supreme Court decision ruled that the 1906 act

---

[1] A History of the FDA at www.FDA.gov.
[2] A History of the FDA at www.FDA.gov.
[3] Text in quotation marks is the original text of the 1906 Food and Drugs Act and Amendments.
[4] A History of the FDA at www.FDA.gov.

---

did not apply to false claims of therapeutic efficacy,[5] in response to which a 1912 amendment added "false and fraudulent" claims of "curative or therapeutic effect" to the Act's definition of "misbranded." However, these powers continued to be narrowly defined by the courts, which set high standards for proof of fraudulent intent.[6] In 1927, the Bureau of Chemistry's regulatory powers were reorganized under a new USDA body, the Food, Drug, and Insecticide organization. This name was shortened to the Food and Drug Administration (FDA) three years later.[7]

The 1938 Food, Drug, and Cosmetic Act

By the 1930s, muckraking journalists, consumer protection organizations, and federal regulators began mounting a campaign for stronger regulatory authority by publicizing a list of injurious products which had been ruled permissible under the 1906 law, including radioactive beverages, cosmetics which caused blindness, and worthless "cures" for diabetes and tuberculosis. The resulting proposed law was unable to get through the Congress of the United States for five years, but was rapidly enacted into law following the public outcry over the 1937 Elixir Sulfanilamide tragedy, in which over 100 people died after using a drug formulated with a toxic, untested solvent. The only way that the FDA could even seize the product was due to a misbranding problem: an "Elixir" was defined as a medication dissolved in ethanol, not the diethylene glycol used in the Elixir Sulfanilamide.

President Franklin Delano Roosevelt signed the new Food, Drug, and Cosmetic Act (FD&C Act) into law on June 24, 1938. The new law significantly increased federal regulatory authority over drugs by mandating a pre-market review of the safety of all new drugs, as well as banning false therapeutic claims in drug labeling without requiring that the FDA prove fraudulent intent. The law also authorized factory inspections and expanded enforcement powers, set new regulatory standards for foods, and brought cosmetics and therapeutic devices under federal regulatory authority. This law, though extensively amended in subsequent years, remains the central foundation of FDA regulatory authority to the present day.[8]

---

[5] United States v. Johnson (31 S. Ct. 627 May 29, 1911, decided).
[6] A History of the FDA at www.FDA.gov.
[7] Milestones in U.S. Food and Drug Law History at www.FDA.gov.
[8] A History of the FDA at www.FDA.gov.

Early FD&C Act amendments: 1938-1958

Soon after passage of the 1938 Act, the FDA began to designate certain drugs as safe for use only under the supervision of a medical professional, and the category of 'prescription-only' drugs was securely codified into law by the 1951 Durham-Humphrey Amendment.[9] While pre-market testing of drug efficacy was not authorized under the 1938 FD&C Act, subsequent amendments such as the Insulin Amendment and Penicillin Amendment did mandate potency testing for formulations of specific lifesaving pharmaceuticals.[10] The FDA began enforcing its new powers against drug manufacturers who could not substantiate the efficacy claims made for their drugs, and the United States Court of Appeals for the Ninth Circuit ruling in Alberty Food Products Co. v. United States (1950) found that drug manufacturers could not evade the "false therapeutic claims" provision of the 1938 act by simply omitting the intended use of a drug from the drug's label. These developments confirmed extensive powers for the FDA to enforce post-marketing recalls of ineffective drugs.[11] Much of the FDA's regulatory attentions in this era were directed towards abuse of amphetamines and barbiturates, but the agency also reviewed some 13,000 new drug applications between 1938 and 1962. While the science of toxicology was in its infancy at the start of this era, rapid advances in experimental assays for food additive and drug safety testing were made during this period by FDA regulators and others.[12]

Good Manufacturing Practices vs. Current Good Manufacturing Practices

The terms "Good Manufacturing Practices (GMPs)" and "Current Good Manufacturing Practices (CGMPs or cGMPs[13])" are often used interchangeably both in industry and by FDA inspectors.

"Good Manufacturing Practices" generally refers to the legal mandates detailed in Title 21 of the Code of Federal Regulations (21CFR). "Current Good Manufacturing Practices" refers not only to the legal

---

[9] A History of the FDA at www.FDA.gov.

[10] Milestones in U.S. Food and Drug Law History at www.FDA.gov

[11] A History of the FDA at www.FDA.gov.

[12] A History of the FDA at www.FDA.gov.

[13] The lower case "c" was coined in industry to differentiate between the law, emphasized with capital letters, and the current accepted industry practice not mandated by law.

---

requirements, but to the guidance provided by the FDA and the standards practiced in industry that are not memorialized as law.

Organizational Structure

The FDA is an agency within the United States Department of Health and Human Services responsible for protecting and promoting the nation's public health. It is organized into the following major subdivisions, each focused on a major area of regulatory responsibility:

- The Office of the Commissioner (OC)
- The Center for Drug Evaluation and Research (CDER)
- The Center for Biologics Evaluation and Research (CBER)
- The Center for Food Safety and Applied Nutrition (CFSAN)
- The Center for Devices and Radiological Health (CDRH)
- The Center for Veterinary Medicine (CVM)
- The National Center for Toxicological Research (NCTR)
- The Office of Regulatory Affairs (ORA)
- The Office of Criminal Investigations (OCI)

How does the FDA communicate with Industry?

Code of Federal Regulations[14]

The Code of Federal Regulations (CFR) is the codification of the general and permanent rules and regulations (sometimes called administrative law) published in the Federal Register by the executive departments and agencies of the Federal Government of the United States. The CFR is published by the Office of the Federal Register, an agency of the National Archives and Records Administration (NARA).

The CFR is divided into 50 titles that represent broad areas subject to Federal regulation. Title 21 is the portion of the Code of Federal Regulations that governs food and drugs within the United States for the Food and Drug Administration (FDA), the Drug Enforcement Administration (DEA), and the Office of National Drug Control Policy (ONDCP).

---

[14] Available CFR Titles on GPO Access at
http://www.access.gpo.gov/nara/cfr/cfr-table-search.html#page1

It is divided into three chapters:

- Chapter I — Food and Drug Administration
- Chapter II — Drug Enforcement Administration
- Chapter III — Office of National Drug Control Policy

Guidance Documents

Guidance documents represent the Agency's current thinking on a particular subject. They do not create or confer any rights for or on any person and do not operate to bind FDA or the public. An alternative approach may be used if such approach satisfies the requirements of the applicable statute, regulations, or both. For information on a specific guidance document, please contact the originating office. Another method of obtaining guidance documents is through the Division of Drug Information.

Federal Register

The Federal Register (since March 14, 1936), abbreviated FR, or sometimes Fed. Reg.) is the official journal of the federal government of the United States that contains most routine publications and public notices of government agencies. It is a daily (except holidays) publication.

The Federal Register is compiled by the Office of the Federal Register (within the National Archives and Records Administration) and is printed by the Government Printing Office.

There are no copyright restrictions on the Federal Register as it is a work of the U.S. government. It is in the public domain.[15]

Citations from the Federal Register are [volume] FR [page number] ([date]), e.g., 65 FR 741 (2000-10-01).

Direct Communication and Letters

The FDA interacts with consumers, health professionals, and industry representatives through letters, meetings (requested by either the FDA or the industry representatives), and telephone calls.

While not all questions can be answered over the phone, the FDA prefers telephone interactions over physical meetings (when a teleconference can reasonably replace a face-to-face meeting).

---

[15] The Federal Register at the GPO, online in both text and PDF, from 1994 on.

www.FDA.gov

The FDA maintains a website at www.fda.gov that is focused on three key audiences:

- consumers
- health professionals
- industry representatives

Through collaboration with users in testing site-wide designs, FDA.gov provides online access to its guidance documents, communication with industry, consumers, and health professionals. Information is categorized by topic, with related subjects consolidated in sections on the site.

Additionally, FDA.gov provides a search engine for Title 21 of the CFR that makes finding keyword references throughout the title more accessible.

Conferences

The FDA routinely sends speakers to industry conferences where they are available to answer questions on their particular area of expertise.

False Statement to a Federal Agency

The U.S. Code of Federal Regulations (CFR) makes it a federal crime for anyone willfully and knowingly to make a false or fraudulent statement to a department or agency of the United States. The false statement must be related to a material matter, and the defendant must have acted willfully and with knowledge of the falsity. It is not necessary to show that the government agency was in fact deceived or misled. The issue of materiality is one of law for the courts. The maximum penalty is five years' imprisonment and a $10,000 fine.

A person may be guilty of a violation without proof that he or she had knowledge that the matter was within the jurisdiction of a federal agency. A businessperson may violate this law by making a false statement to another firm or person with knowledge that the information will be submitted to a government agency. Businesses must take care to avoid exaggerations in the context of any matter that may come within the jurisdiction of a federal agency.

CFR Title 21 - Food and Drugs: Parts 1 to 1499[16]

General

(1) General enforcement regulations

(2) General administrative rulings and decisions

(3) Product jurisdiction

(5) Organization

(7) Enforcement policy

(10) Administrative practices and procedures

(11) Electronic records; electronic signatures

(12) Formal evidentiary public hearing

(13) Public hearing before a public board of inquiry

(14) Public hearing before a public advisory committee

(15) Public hearing before the commissioner

(16) Regulatory hearing before the food and drug administration

(17) Civil money penalties hearings

(19) Standards of conduct and conflicts of interest

(20) Public information

(21) Protection of privacy

(25) Environmental impact considerations

(26) Mutual recognition of pharmaceutical good manufacturing practice

(50) Protection of human subjects

(54) Financial disclosure by clinical investigators

(56) Institutional review boards

(58) Good laboratory practice for nonclinical laboratory studies

(60) Patent term restoration

---

[16] All of the 21CFR regulations can be searched online for no charge at http://www.accessdata.fda.gov/scripts/cdrh/cfdocs/cfcfr/cfrsearch.cfm

---

(70) Color additives

(71) Color additive petitions

(73) Listing of color additives exempt from certification

(74) Listing of color additives subject to certification

(80) Color additive certification

(81) General specifications and general restrictions for provisional color additives for use in foods, drugs, and cosmetics

(82) Listing of certified provisionally listed colors and specifications

(83-98) [reserved]

(99) Dissemination of information on unapproved/new uses for marketed drugs, biologics, and devices

Foods

(100) General

(101) Food labeling

(102) Common or usual name for nonstandardized foods

(104) Nutritional quality guidelines for foods

(105) Foods for special dietary use

(106) Infant formula quality control procedures

(107) Infant formula

(108) Emergency permit control

(109) Unavoidable contaminants in food for human consumption and food-packaging material

(110) Current good manufacturing practice in manufacturing, packing, or holding human food

(111) Current good manufacturing practice in manufacturing, packaging, labeling, or holding operations for dietary supplements

(113) Thermally processed low-acid foods packaged in hermetically sealed containers

(114) Acidified foods

(115) Shell eggs

(119) Dietary supplements that present a significant or unreasonable risk

(120) Hazard analysis and critical control point (HACCP) systems

(123) Fish and fishery products

(129) Processing and bottling of bottled drinking water

(130) Food standards: general

(131) Milk and cream

(133) Cheeses and related cheese products

(135) Frozen desserts

(136) Bakery products

(137) Cereal flours and related products

(139) Macaroni and noodle products

(145) Canned fruits

(146) Canned fruit juices

(150) Fruit butters, jellies, preserves, and related products

(152) Fruit pies

(155) Canned vegetables

(156) Vegetable juices

(158) Frozen vegetables

(160) Eggs and egg products

(161) Fish and shellfish

(163) Cacao products

(164) Tree nut and peanut products

(165) Beverages

(166) Margarine

(168) Sweeteners and table syrups

(169) Food dressings and flavorings

(170) Food additives

(171) Food additive petitions

(172) Food additives permitted for direct addition to food for human consumption

(173) Secondary direct food additives permitted in food for human consumption

(174) Indirect food additives: general

(175) Indirect food additives: adhesives and components of coatings

(176) Indirect food additives: paper and paperboard components

(177) Indirect food additives: polymers

(178) Indirect food additives: adjuvants, production aids, and sanitizers

(179) Irradiation in the production, processing and handling of food

(180) Food additives permitted in food or in contact with food on an interim basis pending additional study

(181) Prior-sanctioned food ingredients

(182) Substances generally recognized as safe

(184) Direct food substances affirmed as generally recognized as safe

(186) Indirect food substances affirmed as generally recognized as safe

(189) Substances prohibited from use in human food

(190) Dietary supplements

(191-199) [reserved]

Drugs

(200) General

(201) Labeling

(202) Prescription drug advertising

(203) Prescription drug marketing

(205) Guidelines for state licensing of wholesale prescription drug distributors

(206) Imprinting of solid oral dosage form drug products for human use

(207) Registration of producers of drugs and listing of drugs in commercial distribution

(208) Medication guides for prescription drug products

(209) Requirement for authorized dispensers and pharmacies to distribute a side effects statement

(210) Current good manufacturing practice in manufacturing, processing, packing, or holding of drugs; general

(211) Current good manufacturing practice for finished pharmaceuticals

(216) Pharmacy compounding

(225) Current good manufacturing practice for medicated feeds

(226) Current good manufacturing practice for type A medicated articles

(250) Special requirements for specific human drugs

(290) Controlled drugs

(299) Drugs; official names and established names

New Drugs and Over-the-Counter Drug Products

(300) General

(310) New drugs

(312) Investigational new drug application

(314) Applications for FDA approval to market a new drug

(315) Diagnostic radiopharmaceuticals

(316) Orphan drugs

(320) Bioavailability and bioequivalence requirements

(328) Over-the-counter drug products intended for oral ingestion that contain alcohol

(330) Over-the-counter (OTC) human drugs which are generally recognized as safe and effective and not misbranded

(331) Antacid products for over-the-counter (OTC) human use

(332) Antiflatulent products for over-the-counter human use

(333) Topical antimicrobial drug products for over-the-counter recognized as safe and effective and not misbranded

(335) Antidiarrheal drug products for over-the-counter human use

(336) Antiemetic drug products for over-the-counter human use

(338) Nighttime sleep-aid drug products for over-the-counter human use

(340) Stimulant drug products for over-the-counter human use

(341) Cold, cough, allergy, bronchodilator, and antiasthmatic drug products for over-the-counter human use

(343) Internal analgesic, antipyretic, and antirheumatic drug products for over-the-counter human use

(344) Topical OTIC drug products for over-the-counter human use

(346) Anorectal drug products for over-the-counter human use

(347) Skin protectant drug products for over-the-counter human use

(348) External analgesic drug products for over-the-counter human use

(349) Ophthalmic drug products for over-the-counter human use

(350) Antiperspirant drug products for over-the-counter human use

(352) Sunscreen drug products for over-the-counter human use [stayed indefinitely]

(355) Anticaries drug products for over-the-counter human use

(357) Miscellaneous internal drug products for over-the-counter human use

(358) Miscellaneous external drug products for over-the-counter human use

(361) Prescription drugs for human use generally recognized as safe and effective and not misbranded: drugs used in research

(369) Interpretative statements re warnings on drugs and devices for over-the-counter sale

(370-499) [reserved]

Veterinary Products

(500) General

(501) Animal food labeling

(502) Common or usual names for nonstandardized animal foods

(509) Unavoidable contaminants in animal food and food-packaging material

(510) New animal drugs

(511) New animal drugs for investigational use

(514) New animal drug applications

(515) Medicated feed mill license

(516) New animal drugs for minor use and minor species

(520) Oral dosage form new animal drugs

(522) Implantation or injectable dosage form new animal drugs

(524) Ophthalmic and topical dosage form new animal drugs

(526) Intramammary dosage forms

(529) Certain other dosage form new animal drugs

(530) Extralabel drug use in animals

(556) Tolerances for residues of new animal drugs in food

(558) New animal drugs for use in animal feeds

(564) [reserved]

(570) Food additives

(571) Food additive petitions

(573) Food additives permitted in feed and drinking water of animals

(579) Irradiation in the production, processing, and handling of animal feed and pet food

(582) Substances generally recognized as safe

(584) Food substances affirmed as generally recognized as safe in feed and drinking water of animals

(589) Substances prohibited from use in animal food or feed

(590-599) [reserved]

Biologics

(600) Biological products: general

(601) Licensing

(606) Current good manufacturing practice for blood and blood components

(607) Establishment registration and product listing for manufacturers of human blood and blood products

(610) General biological products standards

(630) General requirements for blood, blood components, and blood components, and blood derivatives

(640) Additional standards for human blood and blood products

(660) Additional standards for diagnostic substances for laboratory tests

(680) Additional standards for miscellaneous products

Cosmetics

(700) General

(701) Cosmetic labeling

(710) Voluntary registration of cosmetic product establishments

(720) Voluntary filing of cosmetic product ingredient composition statements

(740) Cosmetic product warning statements

(741-799) [reserved]

Medical Devices

(800) General

(801) Labeling

(803) Medical device reporting

(806) Medical devices; reports of corrections and removals

(807) Establishment registration and device listing for manufacturers and initial importers of devices

(808) Exemptions from federal preemption of state and local medical device requirements

(809) In vitro diagnostic products for human use

(810) Medical device recall authority

(812) Investigational device exemptions

(813) [reserved]

(814) Premarket approval of medical devices

(820) Quality system regulation

(821) Medical device tracking requirements

(822) Postmarket surveillance

(860) Medical device classification procedures

(861) Procedures for performance standards development

(862) Clinical chemistry and clinical toxicology devices

(864) Hematology and pathology devices

(866) Immunology and microbiology devices

(868) Anesthesiology devices

(870) Cardiovascular devices

(872) Dental devices

(874) Ear, nose, and throat devices

(876) Gastroenterology-urology devices

(878) General and plastic surgery devices

(880) General hospital and personal use devices

(882) Neurological devices

(884) Obstetrical and gynecological devices

(886) Ophthalmic devices

(888) Orthopedic devices

(890) Physical medicine devices

(892) Radiology devices

(895) Banned devices

(898) Performance standard for electrode lead wires and patient cables

Mammography

(900) Mammography

Radiological Health

(1000) General

(1002) Records and reports

(1003) Notification of defects or failure to comply

(1004) Repurchase, repairs, or replacement of electronic products

(1005) Importation of electronic products

(1010) Performance standards for electronic products: general

(1020) Performance standards for ionizing radiation emitting products

(1030) Performance standards for microwave and radio frequency emitting products

(1040) Performance standards for light-emitting products

(1050) Performance standards for sonic, infrasonic, and ultrasonic radiation-emitting products

Regulations under Certain Other Acts

(1210) Regulations under the federal import milk act

(1230) Regulations under the federal caustic poison act

(1240) Control of communicable diseases

(1250) Interstate conveyance sanitation

(1251-1269) [reserved]

(1270) Human tissue intended for transplantation

(1271) Human cells, tissues, and cellular and tissue-based products

(1272-1299) [reserved]

Controlled Substances

(1300) Definitions

(1301) Registration of manufacturers, distributors, and dispensers of controlled substances

(1302) Labeling and packaging requirements for controlled substances

(1303) Quotas

(1304) Records and reports of registrants

(1305) Orders for schedule I and II controlled substances

(1306) Prescriptions

(1307) Miscellaneous

(1308) Schedules of controlled substances

(1309) Registration of manufacturers, distributors, importers and exporters of List I chemicals

(1310) Records and reports of listed chemicals and certain machines

(1311) Digital certificates

(1312) Importation and exportation of controlled substances

(1313) Importation and exportation of list I and list II chemicals

(1314) Retail sale of scheduled listed chemical products

(1315) Importation and production quotas for ephedrine, pseudoephedrine, and phenylpropanolamine

(1316) Administrative functions, practices, and procedures

Office of National Drug Control Policy

(1400) [reserved]

(1401) Public availability of information

(1402) Mandatory declassification review

(1403) Uniform administrative requirements for grants and cooperative agreements to state and local governments

(1404) Governmentwide debarment and suspension (nonprocurement)

(1405) Governmentwide requirements for drug-free workplace (financial assistance)

(1406-1499) [reserved]

Overview of GCP and Introduction to GLP

Good Clinical Practice

FDA regulates scientific studies that are designed to develop evidence to support the safety and effectiveness of investigational drugs (human and animal), biological products, and medical devices. [17] Physicians and other qualified experts ("clinical investigators") who conduct these studies are required to comply with applicable statutes and regulations. These laws and regulations are intended to ensure the integrity of clinical data on which product approvals are based and to help protect the rights, safety, and welfare of human subjects.

The following resources are provided to help investigators, sponsors, and contract research organizations who conduct clinical studies on investigational new drugs comply with U.S. law and regulations covering good clinical practice (GCP).

General Information

- General Information for Clinical Investigators

- From test-tube to patient: New drug development in the United States

- Information and Activities Targeted Toward Specific Audiences and Populations

Institutional Review Boards (IRBs)

- Institutional Review Boards (IRBs) and Protection of Human Subjects in Clinical Trials

- Guidance for Institutional Review Boards and Clinical Investigators

---

[17] Available on the FDA website at http://www.fda.gov/AboutFDA/CentersOffices/CDER/ucm090259.htm

- FDA Compliance Program 7348.809 - BIMO for Institutional Review Boards

FDA Regulations

- Institutional Review Boards (21 CFR Part 56)

- Human Subject Protection (Informed Consent) (21 CFR Part 50)

- Additional Safeguards for Children involved in Clinical Investigations of FDA-Regulated Products (Interim Rule) (21 CFR Part 50, subpart D)

- Investigational New Drug Application (IND Regulations) (21 CFR Part 312)

Sponsors, Monitors, and Contract Research Organizations

- Guidances and Enforcement Information

- Investigational New Drug Application (IND Regulations) (21 CFR Part 312)

- Regulations for Applications for FDA Approval to Market a New Drug (NDA Regulations) (21 CFR Part 314)

Office of Good Clinical Practice

The Office of Good Clinical Practice[18] is the focal point within FDA for Good Clinical Practice (GCP) and Human Subject Protection (HSP) issues arising in human research trials regulated by FDA. The Office of Good Clinical Practice:

- Advises and assists the Commissioner and other key officials on GCP and HSP issues arising in clinical trials that have an impact on policy, direction, and long-range goals.

- Leads, supports, and administers FDA's Human Subject Protection/Bioresearch Monitoring Council that manages and sets agency policy on bioresearch monitoring (BIMO), GCP, and HSP affecting both clinical and non-clinical trials regulated by FDA. The office also coordinates and provides oversight of working groups established by this Council.

---

[18] Available on the FDA website at
http://www.fda.gov/AboutFDA/CentersOffices/OC/OfficeofScienceandHealth Coordination/GoodClinicalPracticesProgram/default.htm

---

- Coordinates FDA's Bioresearch Monitoring program with respect to clinical trials, working together with all FDA Centers as well as FDA's Office of Regulatory Affairs (ORA)

- Plans and conducts training and outreach programs, both internally and externally.

- Serves as a liaison with other Federal agencies (e.g., the HHS Office for Human Research Protection (OHRP) and the Veterans Administration), outside organizations, regulated industry, and public interest groups on BIMO, GCP, and HSP policies and regulatory matters.

- Contributes to international Good Clinical Practice harmonization activities.

Running Clinical Trials

Adherence to the principles of good clinical practices (GCPs), including adequate human subject protection (HSP) is universally recognized as a critical requirement to the conduct of research involving human subjects. [19] Many countries have adopted GCP principles as laws and/or regulations. The Food and Drug Administration's (FDA's) regulations for the conduct of clinical trials, which have been in effect since the 1970s, address both GCP and HSP. These FDA regulations and guidance documents are accessible from this site. International GCP guidance documents on which FDA has collaborated and that have been adopted as official FDA guidance are also be found here. Finally, this site includes links to other sites relevant to the conduct of clinical trials, both nationally and internationally.

Good Laboratory Practice

The Federal Food, Drug, and Cosmetic Act and Public Health Service Act require that sponsors of FDA-regulated products submit evidence of their product's safety in research and/or marketing applications. These products include food and color additives, animal drugs, human drugs and biological products, human medical devices, diagnostic

---

[19] Available on the FDA website at http://www.fda.gov/ScienceResearch/SpecialTopics/RunningClinicalTrials/defaul t.htm

products, and electronic products.[20] FDA uses the data to answer questions regarding:

- The toxicity profile of the test article.

- The observed no adverse effect dose level in the test system.

- The risks associated with clinical studies involving humans or animals.

- The potential teratogenic, carcinogenic, or other adverse effects of the test article.

- The level of use that can be approved.

The following resources are provided to help investigators, sponsors, and contract research organizations who conduct nonclinical studies on investigational new drugs to comply with U.S. law and regulations covering good laboratory practice (GLP).

- Bioresearch Monitoring: Good Laboratory Practice

- Regulatory Pharmacology and Toxicology

- Toxicological Principles for the Safety of Food Ingredients (Redbook 2000)

- Code of Federal Regulations: Good Laboratory Practice for Nonclinical Laboratory Studies (21 CFR Part 58)

Bioresearch Monitoring

FDA's bioresearch monitoring (BIMO) program conducts on-site inspections of both clinical and nonclinical studies performed to support research and marketing applications/submissions to the agency. Links to the compliance programs for each inspection type and contact information for each Center's BIMO program are also accessible from this site.

Bioresearch Monitoring Program (BIMO)

FDA uses Compliance Program Guidance Manuals (CPGM) to direct its field personnel on the conduct of inspectional and investigational activities. [21] The CPGM's described below form the basis of FDA's

---

[20] Available on the FDA website at: http://www.fda.gov/AboutFDA/CentersOffices/CDER/ucm090275.htm

[21] Available on the FDA website at: http://www.fda.gov/ScienceResearch/SpecialTopics/RunningClinicalTrials/ucm160670.htm

---

Bioresearch Monitoring Program. The purpose of each program is to ensure the protection of research subjects and the integrity of data submitted to the agency in support of a marketing application.

- CPGM for Clinical Investigators
- CPGM for Sponsors, Monitors, and Contract Research Organizations
- CPGM for Good Laboratory Practice (Non-Clinical Laboratories)
- CPGM for In-Vivo Bioequivalence Compliance Program 7348.001
- CPGM for Institutional Review Boards

Bioresearch Monitoring General Information

Program Objectives

The objectives of the bioresearch monitoring program[22] are twofold: (I) to ensure the quality and integrity of data and information submitted in support of investigational and marketing clearance applications or submissions [IDEs, PMAs, and 510(k)s]; and (ii) to ensure that human subjects taking part in investigations are protected from undue hazard or risk. The Division is also charged with the implementation of the FDA's Application Integrity Policy (AIP) for medical devices and radiological health products.

The program objectives are achieved by several means which are discussed in the program functions and inspection program sections below.

Program Functions

The Division of Bioresearch Monitoring's (DBM) operations are directed toward several program areas. These include (1) audits of clinical data contained in PMA and some 510(k) submissions, ordinarily prior to approval; (2) audits of IDE sponsor submissions; (3) inspections of nonclinical laboratories that perform medical device-related safety testing; (4) inspections of Institutional Review Boards that monitor investigational device studies; (5) enforcement of the prohibition against commercialization of investigational devices; (6)

---

[22] Available on the FDA website at: http://www.fda.gov/MedicalDevices/DeviceRegulationandGuidance/Overview/BioresearchMonitoring/ucm052023.htm

providing education, training and guidance to regulated industry and (7) implementation of the FDA's Application Integrity Policy (AIP). Descriptions of some of these activities are summarized below:

- PMA data audits are conducted through comprehensive on-site inspections by FDA field office staff. Source data generated and collected by clinical investigators are compared with the data and information submitted by the sponsor to FDA in support of such applications. These audits help to ensure the quality and integrity of the information used by the FDA to render safety and effectiveness decisions. Additionally, FDA field staff review the appropriate records to ensure protection of the rights and welfare of the clinical research subjects participating in these studies. Where clinical data exists in 510(k) submissions, assignments may be issued requesting audits of that data.

- When indicated, inspections of clinical investigators participating in IDE studies are conducted.

- Good Laboratory Practice (GLP) inspections are undertaken to investigate compliance with regulations promulgated under 21 CFR Part 58, Good Laboratory Practice for Nonclinical Laboratory Studies. Compliance with these regulations is intended to ensure the quality and integrity of safety data obtained from animal studies submitted to FDA.

- Surveillance information received from district offices, the public, the industry, and other sources related to commercialization or promotion of investigational devices is reviewed. If the advertisements or articles deviate from the requirements set forth in 21 CFR 812.7 (Prohibition of promotion and other practices), the Division follows up by means of a letter to the promoter or a request for inspection of the responsible party.

- Implementation of the FDA's Application Integrity Policy involves investigations of sponsors that are suspected of submitting false or misleading data to the FDA. It also includes the review, evaluation, and monitoring of validity assessments required to be completed by sponsors found guilty of fraudulent activities.

The regulations enforced by the bioresearch monitoring program for medical devices are found in four sections of the CFR:

- 21 CFR 812 - Investigational Device Exemptions
- 21 CFR 50 - Protection of Human Subjects

- 21 CFR 56 - Institutional Review Boards

- 21 CFR 58 - Good Laboratory Practice for Nonclinical Laboratory Studies

Inspection Programs

FDA's inspection programs include two types of assignments: routine inspections and directed inspections (sometimes termed "for cause"). The routine assignments include inspections of clinical investigators, sponsors, IRBs, or nonclinical laboratories that are randomly selected for coverage under one of four compliance programs. These assignments are issued to monitor adherence to FDA regulations.

A directed inspection is requested when some specific problem has been identified within one or all entities of the program. The problem may be observed during the review of sponsor submissions related to ongoing IDE investigations or following evaluation of clinical data submitted in a PMA or 510(k) application. Verbal or written complaints from patients, physicians, or competitors may also result in a directed inspection. Inspections issued for PMA data audits also fall into this category.

Deviations revealed during inspections are presented in writing and discussed with the responsible individual at the close of the inspection. Once an inspection has been completed, an establishment inspection report (EIR) is prepared and submitted by the district office. This report is then reviewed and classified by the Division of Bioresearch Monitoring.

Classifications assigned to inspections indicate whether or not the establishment is operating in compliance with the regulations. The classification scheme used by FDA is as follows:

- NAI - No Action Indicated

- VAI - Voluntary Action Indicated

- OAI - Official Action Indicated

Depending upon the assigned classification, the Division may issue an untitled letter or warning letter based upon the severity of the deviations. These letters are intended to communicate the FDA's position on a matter, but do not commit the FDA to take further enforcement action. They are issued for the purpose of achieving voluntary compliance with the expectation that a majority of firms and individuals will comply with the regulations and implement corrective actions to prevent recurrence of the deviations.

When deviations are flagrant or significantly impact the quality and/or integrity of the research data, various actions have been used by the Division to achieve compliance in the bioresearch monitoring program area. Data audits have resulted in the Division's recommendation to invoke the Application Integrity Policy against the sponsor or reject clinical research data used to support a PMA. Data audits for 510(k)s that disclosed improprieties have led the sponsor to withdraw submissions. Monitoring efforts of IDE studies have led to the Division's recommendation for withdrawal of IDEs. Inspections of violative IRBs have resulted in administrative sanctions that suspend the institution's authority to approve new studies and/or add new subjects to existing studies.

Regulations

FDA Regulations Relating to Good Clinical Practice and Clinical Trials

FDA regulations governing the conduct of clinical trials describe good clinical practices (GCPs) for studies with both human and non-human animal subjects.[23]

- Electronic Records; Electronic Signatures (21 CFR Part 11)

- Protection of Human Subjects (Informed Consent) (21 CFR Part 50)

- Financial Disclosure by Clinical Investigators (21 CFR Part 54)

- Institutional Review Boards (21 CFR Part 56)

- FDA IRB Registration Rule (21 CFR 56.106)

- FDA IRB Registration Rule (21 CFR 56.106)

- Good Laboratory Practice for Nonclinical Laboratory Studies (21 CFR Part 58)

- Investigational New Drug Application (21 CFR Part 312)

- Foreign Clinical Trials not conducted under an IND (21 CFR 312.120)

- Expanded Access to Investigational Drugs for Treatment Use

- Charging for Investigational Drugs

---

[23] Available on the FDA website at: http://www.fda.gov/ScienceResearch/SpecialTopics/RunningClinicalTrials/ucm155713.htm#FDARegulations

---

- Form 1571 (Investigational New Drug Application)

- Form 1572 (Statement of Investigator)

- Applications for FDA Approval to Market a New Drug (21 CFR Part 314)

- Bioavailability and Bioequivalence Requirements (21 CFR Part 320)

- New Animal Drugs for Investigational Use (21 CFR Part 511)

- New Animal Drug Applications (21 CFR Part 514)

- Applications for FDA Approval of a Biologic License (21 CFR Part 601)

- Investigational Device Exemptions (21 CFR Part 812)

- Premarket Approval of Medical Devices (21 CFR Part 814)

IDE Enforcement of Good Clinical Practices (GCP) Regulations

Inspection Program

Sponsors, IRBs, and investigators, or any person acting on their behalf, are required to permit authorized FDA employees reasonable access at reasonable times to inspect and copy all records relating to an investigation. Any establishment where devices are held, including any establishment where devices are manufactured, processed, packed, installed, used, or implanted or where records of results from use of devices are kept, are subject to inspection.Furthermore, if FDA has reason to suspect that adequate informed consent was not obtained or that reports required to be submitted by the investigator to the sponsor or IRB have not been submitted or are incomplete, inaccurate, false, or misleading, FDA may inspect and copy records that identify subjects.[24]

To assure compliance with the IDE and related regulations, FDA inspects sponsors, clinical investigators, and institutional review boards. Nonclinical laboratories that perform animal studies in which the data are used to support research or marketing permits are

---

[24] Available on the FDA website at: http://www.fda.gov/MedicalDevices/DeviceRegulationandGuidance/HowtoMarketYourDevice/InvestigationalDeviceExemptionIDE/ucm051363.htm

included in the inspection program. The inspection program is referred to as bioresearch monitoring (BIMO) and is overseen the CDRH's Office of Compliance, Division of Bioresearch Monitoring.

The regulations enforced by the bioresearch monitoring program for medical devices are found in four sections of the CFR:

- 21 CFR 812 - Investigational Device Exemptions

- 21 CFR 50 - Protection of Human Subjects

- 21 CFR 56 - Institutional Review Boards

- 21 CFR 58 - Good Laboratory Practice for Nonclinical Laboratory Studies

The objectives of the bioresearch monitoring program are to ensure the quality and integrity of data and information submitted in support of research and marketing permits that include IDE, PMA, and 510(k) submissions and to ensure that human subjects taking part in investigations are protected from undue hazard or risk. This is achieved through audits of clinical data contained in PMA's prior to approval, data audits of IDE and 510(k) submissions, inspections of Institutional Review Boards and nonclinical laboratories, and enforcement of the prohibition against promotion, marketing, or commercialization of investigational devices.

In addition, the Division is also charged with the implementation of the FDA's Application Integrity Policy (AIP) for medical devices and radiological health products. If it is suspected that an applicant has submitted false or misleading information, the data are thoroughly investigated. Submitting false or misleading information may result in FDA refusal to review submissons until certain requirements are met, as well as the initiation of legal actions.

Disqualification of Clinical Investigators

Disqualification Proceedings

If FDA has information indicating that an investigator has repeatedly or deliberately failed to comply with the IDE, Informed Consent, or IRB requirements under 21 CFR 812, 21 CFR 50, or 21 CFR 56, or has repeatedly or deliberately submitted false information either to the sponsor of the investigation or in any required report, FDA will provide the investigator written notice of the matter under complaint and offer the investigator an opportunity to explain the matter in writing, or, at the option of the investigator, in an informal conference. If an explanation is offered from the investigator and accepted, the disqualification process will be terminated. If an explanation is offered but not accepted, the investigator will be given an opportunity for a regulatory hearing under 21 CFR 16 on the question of whether the investigator is entitled to receive investigational devices.

After evaluating all available information, including any explanation presented by the investigator, if FDA determines that the investigator has repeatedly or deliberately failed to comply with the requirements, or has deliberately or repeatedly submitted false information either to the sponsor of the investigation or in any required report, the FDA will notify the investigator, the sponsor of any investigation in which the investigator has been named as a participant, and the reviewing IRB that the investigator is not entitled to receive investigational devices. The notification will provide a statement of the basis for such determination.

An investigator who has been determined to be ineligible to receive investigational devices may be reinstated as eligible when FDA determines that the investigator has presented adequate assurances that the investigator will employ investigational devices solely in compliance with the IDE and related regulations.

Review of IDE and Marketing Applications

Each investigational device exemption (IDE) and each cleared 510(k) or approved PMA application submitted that contains data reported by an investigator who has been determined to be ineligible to receive investigational devices will be examined to determine whether the investigator has submitted unreliable data that are essential to the continuation of the investigation or essential to the approval or clearance of any marketing application.

FDA will eliminate the unreliable data submitted by the investigator from consideration and review the remaining data. If FDA determines that the remaining data are inadequate to support a conclusion that it is reasonably safe to continue the investigation under IDE, FDA will notify the sponsor who will have an opportunity for a regulatory hearing. If a danger to the public health exists, however, FDA will terminate the IDE immediately and notify the sponsor and the reviewing IRB of the determination. In such a case, the sponsor will have an opportunity for a regulatory hearing before FDA on the question of whether the IDE should be reinstated. If FDA determines from the remaining data that the continued 510(k) clearance or PMA approval of the marketing application for which the data were submitted cannot be justified, FDA will proceed to withdraw approval or rescind clearance of the medical device.

References

- 21 CFR 812.119
- 21 CFR 812.145
- Compliance Program Guidance Manual For FDA Staff
- Bioresearch Monitoring Good Laboratory Practice
- Compliance Program Guidance Manual For FDA Staff - Program 7348.808A
- Institutional Review Boards (IRB) (PDF - 293KB)
- Compliance Program 7348.810 Bioresearch Monitoring
- Bioresearch Monitoring
- Application Integrity Policy
- Disqualified/Restricted/ Restrictions Removed/ Assurance Lists for Clinical Investigators
- Bioresearch Monitoring Agreement for PMAs and PDPs - February 23, 1998
- Integrity of Data and Information Submitted to ODE #I91-2 (blue book memo) (Text Only)
- Bioresearch Monitoring General Information
- FDA Debarment List (Drug Product Applications)
- Public Health Service Administrative Actions Listing

Part I

Federal Regulations Relating to Good Laboratory Practice

Part 58:
Good Laboratory Practice for Nonclinical Laboratory Studies

[Code of Federal Regulations]

[Title 21, Volume 1]

[Revised as of April 1, 2009]

[CITE: 21CFR58]

Title 21--Food and Drugs

Chapter I--Food and Drug Administration

Department of Health and Human Services

Subchapter A--General

Part 58 Good Laboratory Practice for Nonclinical Laboratory Studies[1]

Subpart A--General Provisions

Sec. 58.1 Scope.

(a) This part prescribes good laboratory practices for conducting nonclinical laboratory studies that support or are intended to support applications for research or marketing permits for products regulated by the Food and Drug Administration, including food and color additives, animal food additives, human and animal drugs, medical devices for human use, biological products, and electronic products. Compliance with this part is intended to assure the quality and integrity of the safety data filed pursuant to sections 406, 408, 409, 502, 503, 505, 506, 510, 512-

---

[1] Available on the FDA website at http://www.accessdata.fda.gov/scripts/cdrh/cfdocs/cfcfr/CFRSearch.cfm?CFRPart=58&showFR=1

516, 518-520, 721, and 801 of the Federal Food, Drug, and Cosmetic Act and sections 351 and 354-360F of the Public Health Service Act.

(b) References in this part to regulatory sections of the Code of Federal Regulations are to chapter I of title 21, unless otherwise noted.

[43 FR 60013, Dec. 22, 1978, as amended at 52 FR 33779, Sept. 4, 1987; 64 FR 399, Jan. 5, 1999]

Sec. 58.3 Definitions.

As used in this part, the following terms shall have the meanings specified:

(a) *Act* means the Federal Food, Drug, and Cosmetic Act, as amended (secs. 201-902, 52 Stat. 1040 et seq., as amended (21 U.S.C. 321-392)).

(b) *Test article* means any food additive, color additive, drug, biological product, electronic product, medical device for human use, or any other article subject to regulation under the act or under sections 351 and 354-360F of the Public Health Service Act.

(c) *Control article* means any food additive, color additive, drug, biological product, electronic product, medical device for human use, or any article other than a test article, feed, or water that is administered to the test system in the course of a nonclinical laboratory study for the purpose of establishing a basis for comparison with the test article.

(d) *Nonclinical laboratory study* means in vivo or in vitro experiments in which test articles are studied prospectively in test systems under laboratory conditions to determine their safety. The term does not include studies utilizing human subjects or clinical studies or field trials in animals. The term does not include basic exploratory studies carried out to determine whether a test article has any potential utility or to determine physical or chemical characteristics of a test article.

(e) *Application for research or marketing permit* includes:

(1) A color additive petition, described in part 71.

(2) A food additive petition, described in parts 171 and 571.

(3) Data and information regarding a substance submitted as part of the procedures for establishing that a substance is generally recognized as safe for use, which use results or may reasonably be expected to result, directly or indirectly, in its becoming a component or otherwise affecting the characteristics of any food, described in 170.35 and 570.35.

Part 58

(4) Data and information regarding a food additive submitted as part of the procedures regarding food additives permitted to be used on an interim basis pending additional study, described in 180.1.

(5) Aninvestigational new drug application, described in part 312 of this chapter.

(6) Anew drug application, described in part 314.

(7) Data and information regarding an over-the-counter drug for human use, submitted as part of the procedures for classifying such drugs as generally recognized as safe and effective and not misbranded, described in part 330.

(8) Data and information about a substance submitted as part of the procedures for establishing a tolerance for unavoidable contaminants in food and food-packaging materials, described in parts 109 and 509.

(9) [Reserved]

(10) A Notice of Claimed Investigational Exemption for a New Animal Drug, described in part 511.

(11) A new animal drug application, described in part 514.

(12) [Reserved]

(13) An application for a biologics license, described in part 601 of this chapter.

(14) An application for an investigational device exemption, described in part 812.

(15) An Application for Premarket Approval of a Medical Device, described in section 515 of the act.

(16) A Product Development Protocol for a Medical Device, described in section 515 of the act.

(17) Data and information regarding a medical device submitted as part of the procedures for classifying such devices, described in part 860.

(18) Data and information regarding a medical device submitted as part of the procedures for establishing, amending, or repealing a performance standard for such devices, described in part 861.

(19) Data and information regarding an electronic product submitted as part of the procedures for obtaining an exemption from notification of a radiation safety defect or failure of compliance with a radiation safety performance standard, described in subpart D of part 1003.

(20) Data and information regarding an electronic product submitted as part of the procedures for establishing, amending, or repealing a standard for such product, described in section 358 of the Public Health Service Act.

(21) Data and information regarding an electronic product submitted as part of the procedures for obtaining a variance from any electronic product performance standard as described in 1010.4.

(22) Data and information regarding an electronic product submitted as part of the procedures for granting, amending, or extending an exemption from any electronic product performance standard, as described in 1010.5.

(23) A premarket notification for a food contact substance, described in part 170, subpart D, of this chapter.

(f) *Sponsor* means:

(1) A person who initiates and supports, by provision of financial or other resources, a nonclinical laboratory study;

(2) A person who submits a nonclinical study to the Food and Drug Administration in support of an application for a research or marketing permit; or

(3) A testing facility, if it both initiates and actually conducts the study.

(g) *Testing facility* means a person who actually conducts a nonclinical laboratory study, i.e., actually uses the test article in a test system. Testing facility includes any establishment required to register under section 510 of the act that conducts nonclinical laboratory studies and any consulting laboratory described in section 704 of the act that conducts such studies.Testing facility encompasses only those operational units that are being or have been used to conduct nonclinical laboratory studies.

(h) **Person** includes an individual, partnership, corporation, association, scientific or academic establishment, government agency, or organizational unit thereof, and any other legal entity.

(i) Test system means any animal, plant, microorganism, or subparts thereof to which the test or control article is administered or added for study.Test system also includes appropriate groups or components of the system not treated with the test or control articles.

(j) **Specimen** means any material derived from a test system for examination or analysis.

(k) **Raw data** means any laboratory worksheets, records, memoranda, notes, or exact copies thereof, that are the result of original observations and activities of a nonclinical laboratory study and are necessary for the reconstruction and evaluation of the report of that study. In the event that exact transcripts of raw data have been prepared (e.g., tapes which have been transcribed verbatim, dated, and verified accurate by signature), the exact copy or exact transcript may be substituted for the original source as raw data.Raw data may include photographs, microfilm or microfiche copies, computer printouts, magnetic media, including dictated observations, and recorded data from automated instruments.

(l) **Quality assurance unit** means any person or organizational element, except the study director, designated by testing facility management to perform the duties relating to quality assurance of nonclinical laboratory studies.

(m) **Study director** means the individual responsible for the overall conduct of a nonclinical laboratory study.

(n) **Batch** means a specific quantity or lot of a test or control article that has been characterized according to 58.105(a).

(o) **Study initiation date** means the date the protocol is signed by the study director.

(p) *Study completion date* means the date the final report is signed by the study director.

[43 FR 60013, Dec. 22, 1978, as amended at 52 FR 33779, Sept. 4, 1987; 54 FR 9039, Mar. 3, 1989; 64 FR 56448, Oct. 20, 1999; 67 FR 35729, May 21, 2002]

Sec. 58.10 Applicability to studies performed under grants and contracts.

When a sponsor conducting a nonclinical laboratory study intended to be submitted to or reviewed by the Food and Drug Administration utilizes the services of a consulting laboratory, contractor, or grantee to perform an analysis or other service, it shall notify the consulting laboratory, contractor, or grantee that the service is part of a nonclinical laboratory study that must be conducted in compliance with the provisions of this part.

Sec. 58.15 Inspection of a testing facility.

(a) A testing facility shall permit an authorized employee of the Food and Drug Administration, at reasonable times and in a reasonable manner, to inspect the facility and to inspect (and in the case of records also to copy) all records and specimens required to be maintained regarding studies within the scope of this part. The records inspection and copying requirements shall not apply to quality assurance unit records of findings and problems, or to actions recommended and taken.

(b) The Food and Drug Administration will not consider a nonclinical laboratory study in support of an application for a research or marketing permit if the testing facility refuses to permit inspection. The determination that a nonclinical laboratory study will not be considered in support of an application for a research or marketing permit does not, however, relieve the applicant for such a permit of any obligation under any applicable statute or regulation to submit the results of the study to the Food and Drug Administration.

Subpart B--Organization and Personnel

Sec. 58.29 Personnel.

(a) Each individual engaged in the conduct of or responsible for the supervision of a nonclinical laboratory study shall have education, training, and experience, or combination thereof, to enable that individual to perform the assigned functions.

(b) Each testing facility shall maintain a current summary of training and experience and job description for each individual engaged in or supervising the conduct of a nonclinical laboratory study.

(c) There shall be a sufficient number of personnel for the timely and proper conduct of the study according to the protocol.

(d) Personnel shall take necessary personal sanitation and health precautions designed to avoid contamination of test and control articles and test systems.

(e) Personnel engaged in a nonclinical laboratory study shall wear clothing appropriate for the duties they perform. Such clothing shall be changed as often as necessary to prevent microbiological, radiological, or chemical contamination of test systems and test and control articles.

(f) Any individual found at any time to have an illness that may adversely affect the quality and integrity of the nonclinical laboratory study shall be excluded from direct contact with test systems, test and control articles and any other operation or function that may adversely affect the study until the condition is corrected. All personnel shall be instructed to report to their immediate supervisors any health or medical conditions that may reasonably be considered to have an adverse effect on a nonclinical laboratory study.

Sec. 58.31 Testing facility management.

For each nonclinical laboratory study, testing facility management shall:

(a) Designate a study director as described in 58.33, before the study is initiated.

(b) Replace the study director promptly if it becomes necessary to do so during the conduct of a study.

(c) Assure that there is a quality assurance unit as described in 58.35.

(d) Assure that test and control articles or mixtures have been appropriately tested for identity, strength, purity, stability, and uniformity, as applicable.

(e) Assure that personnel, resources, facilities, equipment, materials, and methodologies are available as scheduled.

(f) Assure that personnel clearly understand the functions they are to perform.

(g) Assure that any deviations from these regulations reported by the quality assurance unit are communicated to the study director and corrective actions are taken and documented.

[43 FR 60013, Dec. 22, 1978, as amended at 52 FR 33780, Sept. 4, 1987]

Sec. 58.33 Study director.

For each nonclinical laboratory study, a scientist or other professional of appropriate education, training, and experience, or combination thereof, shall be identified as the study director. The study director has overall responsibility for the technical conduct of the study, as well as for the interpretation, analysis, documentation and reporting of results, and represents the single point of study control. The study director shall assure that:

(a) The protocol, including any change, is approved as provided by 58.120 and is followed.

(b) All experimental data, including observations of unanticipated responses of the test system are accurately recorded and verified.

(c) Unforeseen circumstances that may affect the quality and integrity of the nonclinical laboratory study are noted when they occur, and corrective action is taken and documented.

(d) Test systems are as specified in the protocol.

(e) All applicable good laboratory practice regulations are followed.

(f) All raw data, documentation, protocols, specimens, and final reports are transferred to the archives during or at the close of the study.

[43 FR 60013, Dec. 22, 1978; 44 FR 17657, Mar. 23, 1979]

Sec. 58.35 Quality assurance unit.

Part 58

(a) A testing facility shall have a quality assurance unit which shall be responsible for monitoring each study to assure management that the facilities, equipment, personnel, methods, practices, records, and controls are in conformance with the regulations in this part. For any given study, the quality assurance unit shall be entirely separate from and independent of the personnel engaged in the direction and conduct of that study.

(b) The quality assurance unit shall:

(1) Maintain a copy of a master schedule sheet of all nonclinical laboratory studies conducted at the testing facility indexed by test article and containing the test system, nature of study, date study was initiated, current status of each study, identity of the sponsor, and name of the study director.

(2) Maintain copies of all protocols pertaining to all nonclinical laboratory studies for which the unit is responsible.

(3) Inspect each nonclinical laboratory study at intervals adequate to assure the integrity of the study and maintain written and properly signed records of each periodic inspection showing the date of the inspection, the study inspected, the phase or segment of the study inspected, the person performing the inspection, findings and problems, action recommended and taken to resolve existing problems, and any scheduled date for reinspection. Any problems found during the course of an inspection which are likely to affect study integrity shall be brought to the attention of the study director and management immediately.

(4) Periodically submit to management and the study director written status reports on each study, noting any problems and the corrective actions taken.

(5) Determine that no deviations from approved protocols or standard operating procedures were made without proper authorization and documentation.

(6) Review the final study report to assure that such report accurately describes the methods and standard operating procedures, and

that the reported results accurately reflect the raw data of the nonclinical laboratory study.

(7) Prepare and sign a statement to be included with the final study report which shall specify the dates inspections were made and findings reported to management and to the study director.

(c) The responsibilities and procedures applicable to the quality assurance unit, the records maintained by the quality assurance unit, and the method of indexing such records shall be in writing and shall be maintained. These items including inspection dates, the study inspected, the phase or segment of the study inspected, and the name of the individual performing the inspection shall be made available for inspection to authorized employees of the Food and Drug Administration.

(d) A designated representative of the Food and Drug Administration shall have access to the written procedures established for the inspection and may request testing facility management to certify that inspections are being implemented, performed, documented, and followed-up in accordance with this paragraph.

[43 FR 60013, Dec. 22, 1978, as amended at 52 FR 33780, Sept. 4, 1987; 67 FR 9585, Mar. 4, 2002]

Subpart C--Facilities

Sec. 58.41 General.

Each testing facility shall be of suitable size and construction to facilitate the proper conduct of nonclinical laboratory studies. It shall be designed so that there is a degree of separation that will prevent any function or activity from having an adverse effect on the study.

[52 FR 33780, Sept. 4, 1987]

Sec. 58.43 Animal care facilities.

(a) A testing facility shall have a sufficient number of animal rooms or areas, as needed, to assure proper: (1) Separation of species or test systems, (2) isolation of individual projects, (3) quarantine of animals, and (4) routine or specialized housing of animals.

(b) A testing facility shall have a number of animal rooms or areas separate from those described in paragraph (a) of this section to ensure isolation of studies being done with test systems or test and control articles known to be biohazardous, including volatile substances, aerosols, radioactive materials, and infectious agents.

(c) Separate areas shall be provided, as appropriate, for the diagnosis, treatment, and control of laboratory animal diseases. These areas shall provide effective isolation for the housing of animals either known or suspected of being diseased, or of being carriers of disease, from other animals.

(d) When animals are housed, facilities shall exist for the collection and disposal of all animal waste and refuse or for safe sanitary storage of waste before removal from the testing facility. Disposal facilities shall be so provided and operated as to minimize vermin infestation, odors, disease hazards, and environmental contamination.

[43 FR 60013, Dec. 22, 1978, as amended at 52 FR 33780, Sept. 4, 1987]

Sec. 58.45 Animal supply facilities.

There shall be storage areas, as needed, for feed, bedding, supplies, and equipment. Storage areas for feed and bedding shall be separated from areas housing the test systems and shall be protected against infestation or contamination. Perishable supplies shall be preserved by appropriate means.

[43 FR 60013, Dec. 22, 1978, as amended at 52 FR 33780, Sept. 4, 1987]

Sec. 58.47 Facilities for handling test and control articles.

(a) As necessary to prevent contamination or mixups, there shall be separate areas for:

(1) Receipt and storage of the test and control articles.

(2) Mixing of the test and control articles with a carrier, e.g., feed.

(3) Storage of the test and control article mixtures.

(b) Storage areas for the test and/or control article and test and control mixtures shall be separate from areas housing the test systems and shall be adequate to preserve the identity, strength, purity, and stability of the articles and mixtures.

Sec. 58.49 Laboratory operation areas.

Separate laboratory space shall be provided, as needed, for the performance of the routine and specialized procedures required by nonclinical laboratory studies.

[52 FR 33780, Sept. 4, 1987]

Sec. 58.51 Specimen and data storage facilities.

Space shall be provided for archives, limited to access by authorized personnel only, for the storage and retrieval of all raw data and specimens from completed studies.

Subpart D--Equipment

Sec. 58.61 Equipment design.

Equipment used in the generation, measurement, or assessment of data and equipment used for facility environmental control shall be of appropriate design and adequate capacity to function according to the protocol and shall be suitably located for operation, inspection, cleaning, and maintenance.

[52 FR 33780, Sept. 4, 1987]

Sec. 58.63 Maintenance and calibration of equipment.

(a) Equipment shall be adequately inspected, cleaned, and maintained. Equipment used for the generation, measurement, or assessment of data shall be adequately tested, calibrated and/or standardized.

(b) The written standard operating procedures required under 58.81(b)(11) shall set forth in sufficient detail the methods, materials, and schedules to be used in the routine inspection, cleaning, maintenance, testing, calibration, and/or standardization of equipment, and shall specify, when appropriate, remedial action to be taken in the event of failure or malfunction of equipment. The written standard operating procedures shall designate the person responsible for the performance of each operation.

(c) Written records shall be maintained of all inspection, maintenance, testing, calibrating and/or standardizing operations. These records, containing the date of the operation, shall describe whether the maintenance operations were routine and followed the written standard operating procedures. Written records shall be kept of nonroutine repairs performed on equipment as a result of failure and malfunction. Such records shall document the nature of the defect, how and when the defect was discovered, and any remedial action taken in response to the defect.

[43 FR 60013, Dec. 22, 1978, as amended at 52 FR 33780, Sept. 4, 1987; 67 FR 9585, Mar. 4, 2002]

Subpart E--Testing Facilities Operation

Sec. 58.81 Standard operating procedures.

(a) A testing facility shall have standard operating procedures in writing setting forth nonclinical laboratory study methods that management is satisfied are adequate to insure the quality and integrity of the data generated in the course of a study. All deviations in a study from standard operating procedures shall be authorized by the study director and shall be documented in the raw data. Significant changes in established standard operating procedures shall be properly authorized in writing by management.

(b) Standard operating procedures shall be established for, but not limited to, the following:

(1) Animal room preparation.

(2) Animal care.

(3) Receipt, identification, storage, handling, mixing, and method of sampling of the test and control articles.

(4) Test system observations.

(5) Laboratory tests.

(6) Handling of animals found moribund or dead during study.

(7) Necropsy of animals or postmortem examination of animals.

(8) Collection and identification of specimens.

(9) Histopathology.

(10) Data handling, storage, and retrieval.

(11) Maintenance and calibration of equipment.

(12) Transfer, proper placement, and identification of animals.

(c) Each laboratory area shall have immediately available laboratory manuals and standard operating procedures relative to the laboratory procedures being performed. Published literature may be used as a supplement to standard operating procedures.

(d) A historical file of standard operating procedures, and all revisions thereof, including the dates of such revisions, shall be maintained.

[43 FR 60013, Dec. 22, 1978, as amended at 52 FR 33780, Sept. 4, 1987]

Sec. 58.83 Reagents and solutions.

All reagents and solutions in the laboratory areas shall be labeled to indicate identity, titer or concentration, storage requirements, and expiration date. Deteriorated or outdated reagents and solutions shall not be used.

Sec. 58.90 Animal care.

(a) There shall be standard operating procedures for the housing, feeding, handling, and care of animals.

(b) All newly received animals from outside sources shall be isolated and their health status shall be evaluated in accordance with acceptable veterinary medical practice.

(c) At the initiation of a nonclinical laboratory study, animals shall be free of any disease or condition that might interfere with the purpose or conduct of the study. If, during the course of the study, the animals contract such a disease or condition, the diseased animals shall be isolated, if necessary. These animals may be treated for disease or signs of disease provided that such treatment does not interfere with the study. The diagnosis, authorizations of treatment, description of treatment, and each date of treatment shall be documented and shall be retained.

(d) Warm-blooded animals, excluding suckling rodents, used in laboratory procedures that require manipulations and observations over an extended period of time or in studies that require the animals to be removed from and returned to their home cages for any reason (e.g., cage cleaning, treatment, etc.), shall receive appropriate identification. All information needed to specifically identify each animal within an animal-housing unit shall appear on the outside of that unit.

(e) Animals of different species shall be housed in separate rooms when necessary. Animals of the same species, but used in different studies, should not ordinarily be housed in the same room when inadvertent exposure to control or test articles or animal mixup could affect the outcome of either study. If such mixed housing is necessary, adequate differentiation by space and identification shall be made.

(f) Animal cages, racks and accessory equipment shall be cleaned and sanitized at appropriate intervals.

(g) Feed and water used for the animals shall be analyzed periodically to ensure that contaminants known to be capable of interfering with the study and reasonably expected to be present in such feed or water are not present at levels above those specified in the protocol. Documentation of such analyses shall be maintained as raw data.

(h) Bedding used in animal cages or pens shall not interfere with the purpose or conduct of the study and shall be changed as often as necessary to keep the animals dry and clean.

(i) If any pest control materials are used, the use shall be documented. Cleaning and pest control materials that interfere with the study shall not be used.

[43 FR 60013, Dec. 22, 1978, as amended at 52 FR 33780, Sept. 4, 1987; 54 FR 15924, Apr. 20, 1989; 56 FR 32088, July 15, 1991; 67 FR 9585, Mar. 4, 2002]

Subpart F--Test and Control Articles

Sec. 58.105 Test and control article characterization.

(a) The identity, strength, purity, and composition or other characteristics which will appropriately define the test or control article shall be determined for each batch and shall be documented. Methods of synthesis, fabrication, or derivation of the test and control articles shall be documented by the sponsor or the testing facility. In those cases where marketed products are used as control articles, such products will be characterized by their labeling.

(b) The stability of each test or control article shall be determined by the testing facility or by the sponsor either: (1) Before study initiation, or (2) concomitantly according to written standard operating procedures, which provide for periodic analysis of each batch.

(c) Each storage container for a test or control article shall be labeled by name, chemical abstract number or code number, batch number, expiration date, if any, and, where appropriate, storage conditions necessary to maintain the identity, strength, purity, and composition of the test or control article. Storage containers shall be assigned to a particular test article for the duration of the study.

(d) For studies of more than 4 weeks' duration, reserve samples from each batch of test and control articles shall be retained for the period of time provided by 58.195.

[43 FR 60013, Dec. 22, 1978, as amended at 52 FR 33781, Sept. 4, 1987; 67 FR 9585, Mar. 4, 2002]

Sec. 58.107 Test and control article handling.

Procedures shall be established for a system for the handling of the test and control articles to ensure that:

(a) There is proper storage.

(b) Distribution is made in a manner designed to preclude the possibility of contamination, deterioration, or damage.

(c) Proper identification is maintained throughout the distribution process.

(d) The receipt and distribution of each batch is documented. Such documentation shall include the date and quantity of each batch distributed or returned.

Sec. 58.113 Mixtures of articles with carriers.

(a) For each test or control article that is mixed with a carrier, tests by appropriate analytical methods shall be conducted:

Part 58

(1) To determine the uniformity of the mixture and to determine, periodically, the concentration of the test or control article in the mixture.

(2) To determine the stability of the test and control articles in the mixture as required by the conditions of the study either:

(i) Before study initiation, or

(ii) Concomitantly according to written standard operating procedures which provide for periodic analysis of the test and control articles in the mixture.

(b) [Reserved]

(c) Where any of the components of the test or control article carrier mixture has an expiration date, that date shall be clearly shown on the container. If more than one component has an expiration date, the earliest date shall be shown.

[43 FR 60013, Dec. 22, 1978, as amended at 45 FR 24865, Apr. 11, 1980; 52 FR 33781, Sept. 4, 1987]

Subpart G--Protocol for and Conduct of a Nonclinical Laboratory Study

Sec. 58.120 Protocol.

(a) Each study shall have an approved written protocol that clearly indicates the objectives and all methods for the conduct of the study. The protocol shall contain, as applicable, the following information:

(1) A descriptive title and statement of the purpose of the study.

(2) Identification of the test and control articles by name, chemical abstract number, or code number.

(3) The name of the sponsor and the name and address of the testing facility at which the study is being conducted.

(4) The number, body weight range, sex, source of supply, species, strain, substrain, and age of the test system.

(5) The procedure for identification of the test system.

(6) A description of the experimental design, including the methods for the control of bias.

(7) A description and/or identification of the diet used in the study as well as solvents, emulsifiers, and/or other materials used to solubilize or suspend the test or control articles before mixing with the carrier. The description shall include specifications for acceptable levels of contaminants that are reasonably expected to be present in the dietary materials and are known to be capable of interfering with the purpose or conduct of the study if present at levels greater than established by the specifications.

(8) Each dosage level, expressed in milligrams per kilogram of body weight or other appropriate units, of the test or control article to be administered and the method and frequency of administration.

(9) The type and frequency of tests, analyses, and measurements to be made.

(10) The records to be maintained.

(11) The date of approval of the protocol by the sponsor and the dated signature of the study director.

(12) A statement of the proposed statistical methods to be used.

(b) All changes in or revisions of an approved protocol and the reasons therefore shall be documented, signed by the study director, dated, and maintained with the protocol.

[43 FR 60013, Dec. 22, 1978, as amended at 52 FR 33781, Sept. 4, 1987; 67 FR 9585, Mar. 4, 2002]

Sec. 58.130 Conduct of a nonclinical laboratory study.

(a) The nonclinical laboratory study shall be conducted in accordance with the protocol.

(b) The test systems shall be monitored in conformity with the protocol.

(c) Specimens shall be identified by test system, study, nature, and date of collection. This information shall be located on the specimen container or shall accompany the specimen in a manner that precludes error in the recording and storage of data.

(d) Records of gross findings for a specimen from postmortem observations should be available to a pathologist when examining that specimen histopathologically.

(e) All data generated during the conduct of a nonclinical laboratory study, except those that are generated by automated data collection systems, shall be recorded directly, promptly, and legibly in ink. All data entries shall be dated on the date of entry and signed or initialed by the person entering the data. Any change in entries shall be made so as not to obscure the original entry, shall indicate the reason for such change, and shall be dated and signed or identified at the time of the change. In automated data collection systems, the individual responsible for direct data input shall be identified at the time of data input. Any change in automated data entries shall be made so as not to obscure the original entry, shall indicate the reason for change, shall be dated, and the responsible individual shall be identified.

[43 FR 60013, Dec. 22, 1978, as amended at 52 FR 33781, Sept. 4, 1987; 67 FR 9585, Mar. 4, 2002]

Subparts H-I [Reserved]

Subpart J--Records and Reports

Sec. 58.185 Reporting of nonclinical laboratory study results.

(a) A final report shall be prepared for each nonclinical laboratory study and shall include, but not necessarily be limited to, the following:

(1) Name and address of the facility performing the study and the dates on which the study was initiated and completed.

(2) Objectives and procedures stated in the approved protocol, including any changes in the original protocol.

(3) Statistical methods employed for analyzing the data.

(4) The test and control articles identified by name, chemical abstracts number or code number, strength, purity, and composition or other appropriate characteristics.

(5) Stability of the test and control articles under the conditions of administration.

(6) A description of the methods used.

(7) A description of the test system used. Where applicable, the final report shall include the number of animals used, sex, body weight range, source of supply, species, strain and substrain, age, and procedure used for identification.

(8) A description of the dosage, dosage regimen, route of administration, and duration.

(9) A description of all cirmcumstances that may have affected the quality or integrity of the data.

(10) The name of the study director, the names of other scientists or professionals, and the names of all supervisory personnel, involved in the study.

(11) A description of the transformations, calculations, or operations performed on the data, a summary and analysis of the data, and a statement of the conclusions drawn from the analysis.

(12) The signed and dated reports of each of the individual scientists or other professionals involved in the study.

(13) The locations where all specimens, raw data, and the final report are to be stored.

(14) The statement prepared and signed by the quality assurance unit as described in 58.35(b)(7).

(b) The final report shall be signed and dated by the study director.

(c) Corrections or additions to a final report shall be in the form of an amendment by the study director. The amendment shall clearly identify that part of the final report that is being added to or corrected and the reasons for the correction or addition, and shall be signed and dated by the person responsible.

[43 FR 60013, Dec. 22, 1978, as amended at 52 FR 33781, Sept. 4, 1987]

Sec. 58.190 Storage and retrieval of records and data.

(a) All raw data, documentation, protocols, final reports, and specimens (except those specimens obtained from mutagenicity tests and wet specimens of blood, urine, feces, and biological fluids) generated as a result of a nonclinical laboratory study shall be retained.

(b) There shall be archives for orderly storage and expedient retrieval of all raw data, documentation, protocols, specimens, and interim and final reports. Conditions of storage shall minimize deterioration of the documents or specimens in accordance with the requirements for the time period of their retention and the nature of the documents or specimens. A testing facility may contract with commercial archives to provide a repository for all material to be retained. Raw data and specimens may be retained elsewhere provided that the archives have specific reference to those other locations.

(c) An individual shall be identified as responsible for the archives.

(d) Only authorized personnel shall enter the archives.

(e) Material retained or referred to in the archives shall be indexed to permit expedient retrieval.

[43 FR 60013, Dec. 22, 1978, as amended at 52 FR 33781, Sept. 4, 1987; 67 FR 9585, Mar. 4, 2002]

Sec. 58.195 Retention of records.

(a) Record retention requirements set forth in this section do not supersede the record retention requirements of any other regulations in this chapter.

(b) Except as provided in paragraph (c) of this section, documentation records, raw data and specimens pertaining to a nonclinical laboratory study and required to be made by this part shall be retained in the archive(s) for whichever of the following periods is shortest:

(1) A period of at least 2 years following the date on which an application for a research or marketing permit, in support of which the results of the nonclinical laboratory study were submitted, is approved by the Food and Drug Administration. This requirement does not apply to studies supporting investigational new drug applications (IND's) or applications for investigational device exemptions (IDE's), records of which shall be governed by the provisions of paragraph (b)(2) of this section.

(2) A period of at least 5 years following the date on which the results of the nonclinical laboratory study are submitted to the Food and Drug Administration in support of an application for a research or marketing permit.

(3) In other situations (e.g., where the nonclinical laboratory study does not result in the submission of the study in support of an application for a research or marketing permit), a period of at least 2 years following the date on which the study is completed, terminated, or discontinued.

(c) Wet specimens (except those specimens obtained from mutagenicity tests and wet specimens of blood, urine, feces, and biological fluids), samples of test or control articles, and specially prepared material, which are relatively fragile and differ markedly in stability and quality during storage, shall be retained only as long as the quality of the preparation affords evaluation. In no case shall retention be required for longer periods than those set forth in paragraphs (a) and (b) of this section.

(d) The master schedule sheet, copies of protocols, and records of quality assurance inspections, as required by 58.35(c) shall be maintained by the quality assurance unit as an easily accessible system of records for the period of time specified in paragraphs (a) and (b) of this section.

(e) Summaries of training and experience and job descriptions required to be maintained by 58.29(b) may be retained along with all other testing facility employment records for the length of time specified in paragraphs (a) and (b) of this section.

(f) Records and reports of the maintenance and calibration and inspection of equipment, as required by 58.63(b) and (c), shall be retained for the length of time specified in paragraph (b) of this section.

(g) Records required by this part may be retained either as original records or as true copies such as photocopies, microfilm, microfiche, or other accurate reproductions of the original records.

(h) If a facility conducting nonclinical testing goes out of business, all raw data, documentation, and other material specified in this section shall be transferred to the archives of the sponsor of the study. The Food and Drug Administration shall be notified in writing of such a transfer.

[43 FR 60013, Dec. 22, 1978, as amended at 52 FR 33781, Sept. 4, 1987; 54 FR 9039, Mar. 3, 1989]

Subpart K--Disqualification of Testing Facilities

Sec. 58.200 Purpose.

(a) The purposes of disqualification are:

    (1) To permit the exclusion from consideration of completed studies that were conducted by a testing facility which has failed to comply with the requirements of the good laboratory practice regulations until it can be adequately demonstrated that such noncompliance did not occur during, or did not affect the validity or acceptability of data generated by, a particular study; and

    (2) To exclude from consideration all studies completed after the date of disqualification until the facility can satisfy the Commissioner that it will conduct studies in compliance with such regulations.

(b) The determination that a nonclinical laboratory study may not be considered in support of an application for a research or marketing permit does not, however, relieve the applicant for such a permit of any obligation under any other applicable regulation to submit the results of the study to the Food and Drug Administration.

Sec. 58.202 Grounds for disqualification.

The Commissioner may disqualify a testing facility upon finding all of the following:

(a) The testing facility failed to comply with one or more of the regulations set forth in this part (or any other regulations regarding such facilities in this chapter);

(b) The noncompliance adversely affected the validity of the nonclinical laboratory studies; and

(c) Other lesser regulatory actions (e.g., warnings or rejection of individual studies) have not been or will probably not be adequate to achieve compliance with the good laboratory practice regulations.

Sec. 58.204 Notice of and opportunity for hearing on proposed disqualification.

(a) Whenever the Commissioner has information indicating that grounds exist under 58.202 which in his opinion justify disqualification of a testing facility, he may issue to the testing facility a written notice proposing that the facility be disqualified.

(b) A hearing on the disqualification shall be conducted in accordance with the requirements for a regulatory hearing set forth in part 16 of this chapter.

Sec. 58.206 Final order on disqualification.

(a) If the Commissioner, after the regulatory hearing, or after the time for requesting a hearing expires without a request being made, upon an evaulation of the administrative record of the disqualification proceeding, makes the findings required in 58.202, he shall issue a final order disqualifying the facility. Such order shall include a statement of the basis for that determination. Upon issuing a final order, the Commissioner shall notify (with a copy of the order) the testing facility of the action.

(b) If the Commissioner, after a regulatory hearing or after the time for requesting a hearing expires without a request being made, upon an evaluation of the administrative record of the disqualification proceeding, does not make the findings required in 58.202, he shall issue a final order terminating the disqualification proceeding. Such order shall include a statement of the basis for that determination. Upon issuing a final order the Commissioner shall notify the testing facility and provide a copy of the order.

Sec. 58.210 Actions upon disqualification.

(a) Once a testing facility has been disqualified, each application for a research or marketing permit, whether approved or not, containing or relying upon any nonclinical laboratory study conducted by the disqualified testing facility may be examined to determine whether such study was or would be essential to a decision. If it is determined that a study was or would be essential, the Food and Drug Administration shall also determine whether the study is acceptable, notwithstanding the disqualification of the facility. Any study done by a testing facility before or after disqualification may be presumed to be unacceptable, and the person relying on the study may be required to establish that the study was not affected by the circumstances that led to the disqualification, e.g., by submitting validating information. If the study is then determined to be unacceptable, such data will be eliminated from consideration in support of the application; and such elimination may serve as new information justifying the termination or withdrawal of approval of the application.

(b) No nonclinical laboratory study begun by a testing facility after the date of the facility's disqualification shall be considered in support of any application for a research or marketing permit, unless the facility has been reinstated under 58.219. The determination that a study may not be considered in support of an application for a research or marketing permit does not, however, relieve the applicant for such a permit of any obligation under any other applicable regulation to submit the results of the study to the Food and Drug Administration.

[43 FR 60013, Dec. 22, 1978, as amended at 59 FR 13200, Mar. 21, 1994]

Sec. 58.213 Public disclosure of information regarding disqualification.

(a) Upon issuance of a final order disqualifying a testing facility under 58.206(a), the Commissioner may notify all or any interested persons. Such notice may be given at the discretion of the Commissioner whenever he believes that such disclosure would further the public interest or would promote compliance with the good laboratory practice regulations set forth in this part. Such notice, if given, shall include a copy of the final order issued under 58.206(a) and shall state that the disqualification constitutes a determination by the Food and Drug Administration that nonclinical laboratory studies performed by the facility will not be considered by the Food and Drug Administration in support of any application for a research or marketing permit. If such notice is sent to another Federal Government agency, the Food and Drug Administration will recommend that the agency also consider whether or not it should accept nonclinical laboratory studies performed by the testing facility. If such notice is sent to any other person, it shall state that it is given because of the relationship between the testing facility and the person being notified and that the Food and Drug Administration is not advising or recommending that any action be taken by the person notified.

(b) A determination that a testing facility has been disqualified and the administrative record regarding such determination are disclosable to the public under part 20 of this chapter.

Sec. 58.215 Alternative or additional actions to disqualification.

(a) Disqualification of a testing facility under this subpart is independent of, and neither in lieu of nor a precondition to, other proceedings or actions authorized by the act. The Food and Drug Administration may, at any time, institute against a testing facility and/or against the sponsor of a nonclinical laboratory study that has been submitted to the Food and Drug Administration any appropriate judicial proceedings (civil or criminal) and any other appropriate regulatory action, in addition to or in lieu of, and prior to, simultaneously with, or subsequent to, disqualification. The Food and Drug Administration may also refer the matter to another Federal, State, or local government law enforcement or regulatory agency for such action as that agency deems appropriate.

(b) The Food and Drug Administration may refuse to consider any particular nonclinical laboratory study in support of an application for a research or marketing permit, if it finds that the study was not conducted in accordance with the good laboratory practice regulations set forth in this part, without disqualifying the testing facility that conducted the study or undertaking other regulatory action.

Sec. 58.217 Suspension or termination of a testing facility by a sponsor.

Termination of a testing facility by a sponsor is independent of, and neither in lieu of nor a precondition to, proceedings or actions authorized by this subpart. If a sponsor terminates or suspends a testing facility from further participation in a nonclinical laboratory study that is being conducted as part of any application for a research or marketing permit that has been submitted to any Center of the Food and Drug Administration (whether approved or not), it shall notify that Center in writing within 15 working days of the action; the notice shall include a statement of the reasons for such action. Suspension or termination of a testing facility by a sponsor does not relieve it of any obligation under any other applicable regulation to submit the results of the study to the Food and Drug Administration.

[43 FR FR 60013, Dec. 22, 1978, as amended at 50 FR 8995, Mar. 6, 1985]

Sec. 58.219 Reinstatement of a disqualified testing facility.

A testing facility that has been disqualified may be reinstated as an acceptable source of nonclinical laboratory studies to be submitted to the Food and Drug Administration if the Commissioner determines, upon an evaluation of the submission of the testing facility, that the facility can adequately assure that it will conduct future nonclinical laboratory studies in compliance with the good laboratory practice regulations set forth in this part and, if any studies are currently being conducted, that the quality and integrity of such studies have not been seriously compromised. A disqualified testing facility that wishes to be so reinstated shall present in writing to the Commissioner reasons why it believes it should be reinstated and a detailed description of the corrective actions it has taken or intends to take to assure that the acts or omissions which led to its disqualification will not recur. The Commissioner may condition reinstatement upon the testing facility being found in compliance with the good laboratory practice regulations upon an inspection. If a testing facility is reinstated, the Commissioner shall so notify the testing facility and all organizations and persons who were notified, under 58.213 of the disqualification of the testing facility. A determination that a testing facility has been reinstated is disclosable to the public under part 20 of this chapter.

Authority: 21 U.S.C. 342, 346, 346a, 348, 351, 352, 353, 355, 360, 360b-360f, 360h-360j, 371, 379e, 381; 42 U.S.C. 216, 262, 263b-263n.

Source: 43 FR 60013, Dec. 22, 1978, unless otherwise noted.

1987 Final Rule - Good Laboratory Practice Regulations

Department of Health and Human Services
Food and Drug Administration
Agency: Food and Drug Administration.

21 CFR Part 58
Good Laboratory Practice Regulations

[Docket No. 83N-0142]

52 FR 33768

September 4, 1987

Action: Final rule.[1]

Summary: *The Food and Drug Administration (FDA) is issuing a final rule that amends the regulations that specify good laboratory practice (GLP) for nonclinical laboratory studies. The amendments clarify, delete, or amend several provisions of the GLP regulations to reduce the regulatory burden on testing facilities. The changes will also achieve a substantial reduction in the paperwork burden imposed upon the regulated industries by the current regulations. Significant changes are made in the provisions respecting quality assurance, protocol preparation, test and control article characterization, and retention of specimens and samples based on FDA's experience in implementing the regulations. The agency has determined that the changes will not compromise the objective of the GLP regulations, which is to assure the quality and integrity of the safety data submitted in support of the approval of regulated products.*

Effective Date: October 5, 1987.

Text: Supplementary Information:

---

[1] Available on the FDA website at: http://www.fda.gov/ICECI/ EnforcementActions/BioresearchMonitoring/NonclinicalLaboratoriesInspectedun derGoodLaboratoryPractices/ucm072706.htm

Background

In the Federal Register of October 29, 1984 (49 FR 43530), FDA published a proposal to amend the agency's regulations in 21 CFR Part 58, which prescribe good laboratory practice for conducting nonclinical laboratory studies (the GLP regulations). The proposal was the result of an evaluation of the GLP regulations and of the data obtained by the agency's inspection program to assess laboratory compliance with the regulations. The evaluation led the agency to conclude that some of the provisions of the regulations could be revised to permit nonclinical testing laboratories greater flexibility in conducting nonclinical laboratory studies without compromising public protection. FDA invited comments on all aspects of the proposal and provided 60 days for interested persons to submit comments, views, data, and information on the need to revise any other provisions of Part 58.

Comments

FDA received 33 comments: 19 from manufacturers of articles regulated by FDA, 4 from associations, 8 from foreign or domestic testing or consulting laboratories, and 2 from individuals within FDA. The majority of these comments endorsed the proposed changes. Many of the comments suggested additional revisions to the GLP regulations or modifications to the proposed changes. A summary of the comments received by FDA during the comment period and the agency's response to them follows.

General

1. One comment urged FDA to initiate training procedures for its field personnel so that the regulated community would obtain maximum benefit from the revisions to the GLP regulations.

    FDA agrees that agency field personnel who conduct inspections of nonclinical testing laboratories need to understand the specific requirements of the GLP regulations to follow appropriate inspectional practices and procedures. FDA has, to date, conducted 17 training courses at its National Center for Toxicological Research in Jefferson, AR, to provide training in good laboratory practice and the associated laboratory inspection techniques. FDA intends to continue to provide such training for its personnel.

2. Eight comments urged FDA to encourage the Environmental Protection Agency (EPA) to adopt similar revisions to its good laboratory practice standards. The comments noted that unless EPA amends its good laboratory practice standards to conform them to FDA's GLP regulations, nonclinical laboratories will still be required to comply with EPA's more stringent requirements. Therefore, regardless of any changes that FDA makes in its regulations, laboratories will not benefit from the revisions unless the EPA regulations are similarly revised.

> FDA recognizes that certain nonclinical laboratories that are subject to FDA's regulations are also subject to the good laboratory practice standards established by EPA under the Federal Insecticide, Fungicide and Rodenticide Act (7 U.S.C. 135 et seq.) and the Toxic Substances Control Act (15 U.S.C. 2600 et seq.). When this final rule becomes effective, some of the provisions of the GLP regulations will differ from the good laboratory practice standards established by EPA. FDA has consulted with EPA officials respecting the changes to FDA's regulations effected by this final rule and will cooperate fully with EPA when that agency propose to revise its regulations.

Scope

3. Except for editorial changes to § 58.1, FDA did not propose to change the scope of Part 58. One comment, however, urged the agency to revise § 58.1 further to make clear that batch release safety tests performed on specific batches of biological products intended for use in clinical trials after tests to establish the basic safety profile have been conducted are subject to the GLP regulations.

> FDA declines to change final § 58.1 on the ground that the studies described by the comment are within the current scope of Part 58. The animal tests performed with an investigational biological product prior to licensing, including the batch release safety tests, are intended to establish the safety of the product. Accordingly, any such test would constitute a nonclinical laboratory study as defined in § 58.3(d). Because such test would also be intended to support a marketing application for a product regulated by FDA, it would be subject to the GLP regulations.

Definitions

4. Four comments endorsed FDA's proposal to change the
    definition of "control article" in § 58.3(c) to exclude from the
    definition feed and water administered to control groups of a test
    system. One comment, however, expressed concern that, by
    relaxing essential standards, the proposed change would
    compromise the quality of the animal test.

    FDA does not agree that excluding feed and water from the
    definition of "control article" will compromise test quality.
    The regulations will continue to contain provisions adequate
    to control the use of feed and water in a nonclinical
    laboratory study. For example, § 58.31(e) requires
    management to assure that materials are available as
    scheduled, § 58.45 provides for proper feed storage, §
    58.81(b)(2) requires the preparation of standard operating
    procedures for animal care (e.g., nutrition), § 58.90(g) requires
    periodic analysis of feed and water for interfering
    contaminants, and final § 58.120(a)(7) (formerly §
    58.120(a)(9)) requires the protocol to contain a description or
    an identification of the diet, including specifications for
    acceptable levels of contaminants. Other sections of the
    regulations also apply to feed or water that is used as a carrier
    for the test or control article. For example, § 58.31(d) requires
    management to assure that test and control article mixtures
    have been appropriately tested, § 58.47 requires that a testing
    facility include storage areas that are adequate to preserve the
    identity, strength, purity, and stability of such mixtures, and §
    58.113 requires the laboratory to conduct appropriate
    analyses for uniformity of the mixture, as well as
    concentration and stability of the test article in the mixture.
    As discussed at length in the preamble to the proposal (49 FR
    43531), the amendment to § 58.3(c) will mean that the feed
    and water provided to the control groups of a test system will
    not be subject to certain provisions of the regulations, e.g.,
    those requiring control articles to be characterized and tested
    for stability (§ 58.105), retained as reserve samples (§ 58.195),
    or accountable with respect to use (§ 58.107). As discussed
    above, however, the regulations will continue to require the
    provision of adequate supplies of feed and water, a
    description of the feed, proper storage, and use accountability
    procedures as directed by the protocol, and standard
    operating procedures. Further, only feed and water shown to

be free from unacceptable contamination may be used in a study.

For the reasons above, FDA concludes that the change to § 58.3(c) will not compromise the quality of the animal test and that the term "control article" should be reserved for the discrete substances/articles and vehicles other than feed and water administered to groups of the test system to provide a basis of comparison with the test article.

5. Four comments on proposed § 58.3(d) endorsed FDA's proposal to allow laboratories to conduct several experiments using the same test article under a single, comprehensive protocol. One comment, however, expressed concern that by amending the definition of "nonclinical laboratory study," FDA may inadvertently encourage laboratories to establish protocols that (1) are too brief to assure the quality and integrity of safety data developed through a study conducted under the protocol, or (2) do not describe study procedures in sufficient detail for such assurance, because lengthy "umbrella protocols" may be difficult to administer and track during the amendment process.

Under the revised definition in § 58.3(d), a single "umbrella" protocol may be used for concurrent testing of more than one test article using a single common procedure, e.g., mutagenicity testing, or for a battery of studies of one test article conducted in several test systems. Section 58.120 requires that each study have an approved written protocol that clearly indicates the objectives and all methods for the conduct of the study, and § 58.33 requires the study director to assure that the protocol is approved and followed.

FDA notes that the changed definition of "nonclinical laboratory study" does not require any laboratory to establish "umbrella" protocols -- it only allows it as an option. The agency recognizes that a longer, more complex protocol might be more difficult to manage than a simpler one; however, using an "umbrella" protocol should be more efficient than using several closely related protocols. The quality or accuracy of test data and procedures should not be compromised, while the paperwork burden should be reduced. In any event, the laboratory remains responsible for assuring that the validity of any study that it conducts is not adversely affected due to an inadequate protocol.

6. One comment urged FDA to revise further the definition of nonclinical laboratory study to define the terms "study initiation" and "study termination."

> FDA recognizes that differing words and phrases are used within the GLP regulations to denote dates respecting significant events that occur during a laboratory study. For this reason, the agency agrees that it may be useful to add to the regulations definitions of the terms "study initiation" and "study completion."

> FDA advises that the study initiation date represents the date on which the study director has completed plans in preparation for the technical conduct of a study (see § 58.33) and on which, under § 58.31(e), management is required to make certain that personnel, resources, facilities, equipment, materials, and methodologies for the study are available as scheduled. On the study initiation date, the study is entered on the master schedule sheet (see § 58.35(b)(1)). After this date, any protocol changes are to be made only in accordance with the procedure described in § 58.120(b). Accordingly, FDA is adding new § 58.3(o) to define "study initiation" to mean the date the protocol is signed by the study director.

> The study completion date is the date on which the study director signs the final report (see final § 58.185(b)). On the study completion date, the study director is required to make certain that raw data, documentation, protocols, specimens, and final reports are transferred to the archives (see § 58.33(f)), and under § 58.35, the quality assurance unit may retire the study from the master schedule sheet. This date also specifies the beginning of the record retention period under § 58.195(b). After the study completion date, final reports may be amended only in accordance with the procedure described in § 58.185(c). Accordingly, FDA is adding new § 58.3(p) to define "study completion" to mean the date the final report is signed by the study director. As a necessary conforming amendment, FDA is also amending § 58.185(b) to provide that the final report shall contain the dated signature of the study director.

> FDA advises that the phrase "close of the study" as used in § 58.33(f) refers to the study completion date. Also, the terms "terminate" and "discontinue" as used in § 58.195(b)(3) are used in their ordinary senses to mean stop, cease, break off,

or give up, denoting that a study has been ended before the planned study completion date. For these reasons, FDA believes that these terms do not need any further definition to make clear their meanings.

7a. Three comments urged FDA to expand the definition of "raw data" under § 58.3(k) to provide that the computer record of "hand-recorded data entered into the computer verbatim and verified" could be substituted for the original source as raw data.

FDA does not agree that the computer record of hand-recorded data may be considered as raw data. Individuals who enter data from a laboratory study into the computer commonly do not have any knowledge of the conditions under which the data were collected and may not understand the data originator's notations that regularly are included on the hand-recorded data sheets. The probability of error in data entry is greatly increased under these circumstances.

7b. One comment urged the agency to revise § 58.3(k) to make clear that the term "raw data" as it pertains to the findings of the histopathological examinations refers only to the signed and dated final report of the pathologist.

FDA does not agree that it needs to amend the definition of raw data relative to the findings of histopathological examinations. In pertinent part, § 58.3(k) defines raw data as laboratory worksheets, records, memoranda, notes, or exact copies thereof, that are the result of original observations and activities and are necessary for the reconstruction and evaluation of the final report. Although the notes taken by a pathologist during histopathological examination of slides are indeed the result of original observations, these notes are not necessary for the reconstruction and evaluation of the final report. The final report is evaluated by an analysis of the pathology syndrome as described in the pathologist's report, which is required under § 58.185(a)(12). Further, because § 58.190(a) requires histopathological blocks, tissues, and slides to be retained as specimens, the final report can be reconstructed by verification of the pathology findings by, e.g., a second pathologist or by a team of pathologists.

The pathologist's interim notes, therefore, which are subject to frequent changes as the pathologist refines the diagnosis,

1987 Final Rule

are not raw data because they do not contribute to study reconstruction. Accordingly, only the signed and dated final report of the pathologist comprises raw data respecting the histopathological evaluation of tissue specimens.

Testing Facility Management

8. One comment objected to FDA's proposal to delete the provision in § 58.31(b) that requires testing facility management to document as "raw data" the replacement of a study director. The comment argued that it could be difficult to retrieve such documentation if data were transferred to another location after completion of a study.

    FDA proposed to delete the requirement in § 58.31(b) to document study director replacement as "raw data" in the agency's belief that other provisions of the GLP regulations adequately require documentation of this event. The agency continues to believe that the requirement in § 58.31(b) is redundant to such other provisions and is not necessary to assure the quality and integrity of the safety data developed through a study conducted by a laboratory. For example, § 58.35(b)(1) provides that the master schedule sheet shall contain the name of the study director. Thus, replacement of the study director would necessitate an updating of the master schedule sheet. The master schedule sheet itself is "raw data" because it is a record that is the result of laboratory activities and is necessary for the reconstruction of the study. Also, § 58.120(b) requires that any change in an approved protocol and the reason or reasons for the change are to be documented. Because § 58.120(a)(11) of the final rule (previously § 58.120(a)(15)) requires that the protocol contain the dated signature of the study director, replacement of the study director would constitute such a change. Other provisions of the regulations require the quality assurance unit to retain the master schedule sheet and copies of protocols as an easily accessible system of records for a specified period after completion of the study (§ 58.195(d)). Therefore, it should not be difficult to identify the term of each study director even if records are transferred elsewhere after study completion.

Study Director

9. Several comments objected to § 58.33 in its entirety on the grounds that (1) the regulation does not clearly define the responsibility of the study director and (2) the wording of the regulation implies that the study director must be technically competent in all areas of a study. One comment argued that the study director should be responsible only for "coordinating" the technical conduct, interpretation, analysis, documentation, and reporting of results.

> FDA discussed at length in the preamble to the GLP final rule the intent of § 58.33 and the requirements applicable to the individual who is designated the study director for any study (43 FR 59986, 59995; December 22, 1978). As discussed in that preamble, the study director represents the single, fixed point of responsibility for overall conduct of each study. Although "coordination" of the pieces of a study logically is part of the study director's responsibilities, to limit his or her responsibilities to mere "coordination" would compromise public protection if another person were not such designated fixed point and would add an unnecessary burden if FDA were to require a laboratory to employ an additional person to provide such a point. The study director is charged with the technical conduct of a study, including interpretation, analysis, documentation, and reporting of results. FDA does not intend, however, that the individual is to be technically competent in all areas of a study. FDA's inspectional experiences have demonstrated that if responsibility for proper study conduct is not assigned to one person, a potential exists for the issuance of conflicting instructions and improper protocol implementation.

> FDA concludes that the comments did not provide any new data or information to negate the agency's original determinations and that it should retain § 58.33 as it was established in the December 22, 1978, final rule.

10. One comment objected to FDA's proposal to delete the phrase "and verified" from § 58.33(b), which currently requires that the study director assure that all experimental data are "verified" as well as accurately recorded. The comment argued that removing the study director's obligation to assure that the data have been verified would dilute the responsibility of the study director for proper conduct of the study.

FDA has carefully reevaluated its proposal to remove the phrase "and verified" from § 58.33(b). FDA proposed to delete the phrase from the regulation in response to arguments from management of testing facilities that they misinterpreted the provision, apparently believing that it required the study director personally to witness each data observation. FDA did not intend the provision to so require. Rather, the agency regards the study director as responsible for assuring that all experimental data are verified.

Ordinarily the verification required by § 58.33(b) is obtained by the individual collecting the data, using data verification procedures described in the protocol or in the specific standard operating procedure, and by the individual's supervisor as part of the supervisory quality control procedures. "Verified" is used to describe the study director's responsibility to assure the accurate recording of data. Verification in this sense does not require the study director to observe every data collection event but does require the study director to make certain that the study conduct procedures designated in the protocol for a study and the standard operating procedures established for a study are followed. For all these reasons, FDA has decided to retain the phrase "and verified" to confirm the need for data verification in nonclinical laboratory studies.

11. Two comments urged that the study director's responsibility for assuring placement in the archives of the study records specified under § 58.33(f) be transferred to testing facility management under § 58.31. The comments argued that raw data and documentation are under the immediate control of facility management rather than the study director.

The change suggested by the comments would conflict with the study director's responsibility identified in § 58.33 of representing the single point of study control (see paragraph 9 of this preamble). The archived materials of each study, including raw data and documentation, constitute lasting proof of study validity. The transfer of such materials to the archives is a critical step in study control that assures that the archived materials are complete and adequate for study reconstruction. Indeed, these revised regulations further emphasize the study director's control function by defining the study completion date as the date the final report is signed and dated by the study director; after this date, the study director assures that all required materials are transferred to the archives. Consequently, FDA declines to accept the change proposed by the comments.

Quality Assurance Unit

12. FDA received eight comments regarding § 58.35(a), which sets forth the composition and function of the Quality Assurance Unit (QAU). One comment endorsed FDA's proposal to substitute "which" for the current phrase, "composed of one or more individuals who," to make clear the personnel who can perform quality assurance duties. The comment suggested, however, that the agency use the term "function" or "activity" in § 58.35(a) in place of the current term "unit" to make it clear that quality assurance monitoring need not be performed by individuals of a permanently staffed unit. Four comments disagreed strongly with the proposed change to § 58.35(a), arguing that the change inappropriately implies that assurance of a well-conducted study does not require special training or experience. The comments also asserted that verifiable data are produced as a result of the current requirement for an independent, fixed and permanently staffed quality assurance unit. Other comments argued that individuals should not monitor studies similar to their own work. Some comments requested further clarification of the required composition of the QAU.

FDA does not believe that identification of the quality assurance unit as a "function" or "activity" would serve to clarify the composition or function of the QAU. FDA never has intended that the QAU necessarily has to be a separate entity or a permanently staffed "unit" (see 43 FR 59996). "Quality assurance unit" has become an accepted term to describe those individuals responsible for quality assurance as described in § 58.35. FDA also does not agree that the proposed revision to § 58.35(a) implies that assurance of a well-conducted study does not require special training or experience on the part of individuals monitoring the conduct and reporting of a nonclinical laboratory study. FDA continues to believe that well-qualified and trained personnel are essential to quality assurance under the GLP regulations and that one of management's most important responsibilities in maintaining effective quality assurance is to provide an adequate number of such personnel (§ 58.31 (c) and (e)).

1987 Final Rule

FDA concludes from the comments that the requirements set forth in § 58.35(a) have been misinterpreted in some instances to mean that the regulations require that the QAU be composed of individuals whose sole duties are in quality assurance. In fact, the agency intends only that quality assurance activities be separated from study direction and conduct activities; that is, a trained and qualified person who works on one study can perform quality assurance duties on any study in which he or she is not involved. FDA's reason for requiring separation of quality assurance functions from study conduct functions is fundamental -- to assure that quality assurance personnel can act candidly, without bias or a real or perceived conflict of interest. In effecting the separation required by the GLP regulations, FDA was aware that many small laboratories could not afford the operation of a permanently staffed QAU. For this reason, the agency concluded that the separation of functions on a study-by-study basis as permitted in the existing and revised regulations would provide effective quality assurance. The agency's intent in defining the composition and function of the QAU was discussed at length in the preamble to the current GLP regulations (see 43 FR 59996). FDA believes that the change now being made more clearly reflects the agency's original intent.

13. One comment recommended that FDA delete the word "sheet" from the term "master schedule sheet" in § 58.35(b)(1) on the ground that there are methods for maintaining a master schedule other than use of an actual "sheet."

FDA acknowledges that current technology allows for various methods for maintaining a master schedule, ranging from sophisticated computerized procedures to procedures whereby such information is contained in written records. Regardless of the method utilized, however, the master schedule information is "raw data" within the meaning of the GLP regulations and copies of the master schedule are required to be retained in the study archives in accordance with § 58.195(b). The agency is, therefore, retaining the term "master schedule sheet" to emphasize that the master schedule constitutes raw data subject to agency inspection and that the records must be retained.

14. One comment suggested that FDA delete the current provision in § 58.35(b)(1), which requires a laboratory to include the name of

the sponsor of each study on the master schedule sheet for all studies conducted at the facility. The comment urged the agency to allow sponsor identification by code.

FDA agrees that including the sponsors' name on the master schedule sheet is not essential either for the conduct of management's functions listed in § 58.31 or for the conduct of proper quality assurance under § 58.35. Sponsor identification by code is an adequate procedure, provided that the name of any sponsor is made available to FDA upon request. Accordingly, FDA is amending § 58.35(b)(1) to read "* * * identity of the sponsor * * *."

15. One comment suggested that FDA further revise § 58.35(b)(1) to allow the master schedule sheet to be indexed by study number rather than test article on the ground that multiple studies may be performed on each test article.

FDA recognizes that a nonclinical laboratory may have in progress several studies on each test article that is listed on the master schedule sheet. The agency concludes, however, that indexing by study number alone and not by test article would be inappropriate. The master schedule sheet is the mechanism through which the QAU can assure management that the facilities are adequate and that there are sufficient numbers of qualified personnel available to accomplish the scheduled work (see 43 FR 59997). In addition, § 58.31(e) requires management to assure that study materials (e.g., test articles) are available as scheduled. The use of study numbers rather than test articles as index terms would, therefore, frustrate a major purpose of the master schedule sheet and impede the conduct of an important management function.

16. Three comments endorsed FDA's proposal to delete the current requirement under § 58.35(b)(1) that the status of the final report be a distinct entry on the master schedule sheet. One comment, however, objected to the proposal on the basis that frequently there are delays in completing the final report, and the study status often is different from the expected date of completion of the report.

FDA believes that the comment that objected to the proposal misconstrued the purpose of revising § 58.35(b)(1). Section 58.35(b)(1) currently requires that the master schedule sheet contain separate headings for the "current status" of the

1987 Final Rule

study and for the "status of the final report" of the study. FDA considers the preparation of the final report to be a study event, current status of which should be reflected on the master schedule sheet. Preparation of the final report is similar to other study events (e.g., test article-mixture preparation, test system dosing, in life observations) that are listed under "current status." Under this revision to § 58.35(b)(1), the master schedule sheet would contain the same information respecting the final report as is required under the current GLP regulations, but the information would be included only under the "current status" heading. The agency advises that "expected date of completion of a final report" is not a "status" entry. Such information has not been required in the past nor is this information being required now.

17. FDA proposed to revise § 58.35(b)(3) to provide specifically that the QAU need only inspect "each nonclinical laboratory study" on a schedule adequate to assure the integrity of the study. Four comments recommended that the agency further revise the regulation to substitute the word "studies" for the phrase "each nonclinical laboratory study" alleging that inspection of multiple short duration studies can result in expenditure of significant time and effort with little derived benefit. Two comments argued that inspection of short duration studies conducted repeatedly at the same facility by the same personnel is not necessary and suggested that, in lieu of requiring inspection of each study, standard operating procedures be developed to determine the inspection frequency of various types of studies. These comments also recommended that such inspections be used to demonstrate compliance of other similar studies conducted in the same time frame.

> FDA does not agree with the comments. The quality of each nonclinical laboratory study submitted to the agency in support of an application for a research or marketing permit for a product regulated by FDA is critical to a determination of the safety of the product. The principle of quality assurance advanced in the GLP regulations is to inspect studies to identify and correct problems in a timely fashion. FDA is convinced that such problems can be detected only through a program of vigorous inspection of each study. This does not mean, however, that every phase of every study

needs to be inspected by the QAU (see paragraph 18 of this preamble).

18. Two comments disagreed with FDA's proposal to modify the current requirement in § 58.35(b)(3) that the QAU inspect each phase of a study at specified intervals. The comments argued that elimination of specified quality assurance inspection intervals may result in decreased compliance by cost-cutting laboratories. Another comment urged FDA to identify the critical phases of a nonclinical laboratory study to be inspected by the QAU.

Section 58.35(b)(3) currently provides that the QAU is to inspect at periodic intervals each phase of a nonclinical laboratory study. For studies lasting more than 6 months, the inspections are to be conducted every 3 months. For studies lasting less than 6 months, the inspections are to be conducted at intervals adequate to assure the integrity of the study (including each phase at least once). The term "each phase" was intended to emphasize the need for repeated surveillance so that the QAU observes at least once during the course of the study each critical operation. The term "periodic" was included in the regulation to indicate the need for more than one inspection of certain repetitive, continuing operations. In light of current information, however, FDA does not believe that such a rigid schedule is essential to assure study quality. The agency has learned through its inspection program that the quality of toxicology testing is much higher than that envisioned in 1976 when FDA proposed to establish the GLP regulations (see 41 FR 51206, 51207-51208; November 19, 1976).

Contemporary concepts of quality assurance emphasize the effectiveness of thorough, in-depth inspections of study processes (i.e., all operations required to accomplish a study phase) in place of quick, spot checks of individual operations with a study. Thorough examination of personnel, facilities, equipment, standard operating procedures, data collection procedures, raw data books, and other features associated with a study phase can achieve more effective quality assurance than does a more superficial observation of the conduct of the same study phase in a series of studies.

The agency has concluded that the QAU's inspection schedule should take into account the need for inspection of each study on a schedule adequate to assure the integrity of the study being monitored. The change in § 58.35(b)(3) permits the QAU to exercise reasonable flexibility and judgment so that inspections can be scheduled to best achieve the goal of assuring that studies are properly conducted. The agency advises, however, that each study, no matter how short, needs to be inspected in-process at least once. Further, across a series of studies all phases should be inspected in order to assure the integrity of the studies. For these reasons, FDA does not believe that the regulation as revised will result in decreased compliance with the GLP regulations or that the term "critical phase" needs to be defined.

19. Eight comments addressed FDA's proposal to delete § 58.35(b)(4), which currently requires the QAU to submit periodic written status reports to management and to the study director. One of the comments supported the proposal on the basis that the provisions of § 58.35(b)(3), which require reports to management on problems likely to affect study integrity, are adequate to assure study quality. Several comments questioned whether deleting § 58.35(b)(4) would provide any practical benefit to testing facilities, noting that management is likely to continue to expect periodic reports. One comment noted that elimination of the requirement for status reports could allow management to disregard quality assurance problems if management is only marginally supportive of good laboratory practice and quality assurance. Three comments argued that, by deleting the provision, FDA would inappropriately place on the QAU rather than on the study director the obligation of determining what constitutes a problem likely to affect the integrity of a study. One comment argued that, because management is required to be involved in corrective actions under the provisions of §§ 58.31(g) and 58.35(b)(3), management must be kept informed respecting the status and the progress of any study inspected by the QAU. Another comment suggested that FDA delete the requirement that status reports be provided to the study director but retain the requirement that management receive such reports.

After careful consideration of these comments, FDA has concluded that § 58.35(b)(4) should be retained in its current form. The agency proposed to delete the paragraph based on its tentative conclusion that routine reports of unremarkable findings by the QAU are not essential to study quality. The comments, however, are persuasive in that such reports are necessary to demonstrate to management that the QAU is functioning properly. It is also necessary that the study director continue to receive such reports because that individual is responsible for all aspects of any study being conducted by a facility, including GLP compliance.

20. One comment suggested that, in lieu of deleting the entire paragraph, § 58.35(b)(4) be modified by removing the requirement for status reports on each study, thereby reducing paperwork.

   In accord with the conclusions stated in paragraph 19 of this preamble, FDA believes that it is inappropriate to eliminate the requirement for status reports for each study. Without status reports on each study, there would not be adequate assurances concerning the quality of the ongoing studies.

21. One comment urged FDA to revise current § 58.35(b)(5) to hold the QAU responsible only to (1) determine that known deviations from approved protocols or standard operating procedures were not made without proper documentation, and (2) require authorization for anticipated deviations. The comment argued that the current wording of the regulation implies that the QAU shall have prior knowledge of any deviations and shall approve such deviations, which is not the case in most instances.

   FDA would not consider a laboratory to have violated § 58.35(b)(5) if a deviation was not authorized in advance because it was unanticipated. For example, as recognized in the preamble to the final rule (43 FR 59998), a fire in the facility would necessitate immediate action. Also, as discussed at length at 43 FR 59998, FDA does not intend that the QAU is responsible for authorizing any deviations from the protocol or standard operating procedures, rather it is responsible for detecting any such deviations by its inspection and audit procedures. The revision suggested by the comment would remove the accountability of the QAU for detecting deviations and would undermine the requirements for quality assurance.

22. FDA proposed to revise current § 58.35(b)(7) to provide that the statement which the QAU prepares to accompany the final report would be required to identify the phases of the study inspected and the number of inspections conducted. Eleven comments objected to the proposed change to the regulation, which currently requires only that the statement by the QAU specify the dates that inspections of the study were made and the dates that findings

were reported to management and to the study director. Most of the comments were concerned with the additional reporting burden imposed by the proposed revision. Some of the comments argued that the information sought by FDA through the proposed revision in § 58.35(b)(7) is currently required under the provisions of § 58.35 (b)(3) and (c). These comments pointed out that requiring additional documentation would be duplicative and contrary to the stated purposes of the proposed revisions to the GLP regulations.

FDA has carefully reevaluated its proposal to require that the QAU statement identify the phases of a study inspected and the number of inspections conducted. The agency is persuaded that the proposal would have provided information redundant to that which is available under other provisions of the GLP regulations. Accordingly, FDA has decided not to change § 58.35(b)(7) and is retaining this provision in its current form. Proposed § 58.35(b)(6) (as § 58.35(b)(7) would have been renumbered) is not being adopted.

Animal Care Facilities

23. One comment objected to the proposed modification to § 58.43(c), which would delete the current requirement that all laboratory facilities include separate areas for the diagnosis, treatment, and control of laboratory animal diseases. The comment noted that animal health is a major problem in toxicology testing. For this reason, the comment argued that any relaxation of the current requirements in the GLP regulations for animal care is ill-advised and contradictory to FDA's responsibility for the welfare of animals.

As discussed in the preamble to the proposed amendments to the GLP regulations (49 FR 43532), a laboratory may elect to dispose of diseased animals, thereby obviating the need for dedicated areas for such animals. FDA believes that it is not cost-effective to require separate areas in every case and has concluded that the decision concerning appropriate separation of animals should be made by the study director in consultation with other scientific personnel. The agency does not believe that providing for dedicated laboratory areas as appropriate compromises FDA's continuing commitment to animal welfare, which is specifically dealt with in § 58.90.

Indeed, FDA believes that the GLP regulations foster quality animal testing under defined conditions so that fewer animals are required to establish product safety.

Animal Supply Facilities

24. FDA proposed to revise § 58.45 to permit laboratories to store perishable supplies or feed by methods most appropriate to the characteristics of the materials. One comment urged FDA to amend § 58.45 further to permit storage of animal feed in rooms housing small animals or small groups of animals that are isolated from other studies.

> FDA declines to amend § 58.45 as recommended by the comment. In developing the current GLP regulations, the agency carefully considered whether animal feed or bedding might be stored within any test areas. FDA concluded at that time that storage areas needed for feed and bedding should be separate from the areas housing the test system to preclude mixups and contamination of test article-carrier mixtures and inadvertent exposure of the test system to potentially interfering contaminants. FDA continues to believe that separate storage areas for feed and animal bedding should be required and the comment did not provide any data to counter this belief. FDA advises, however, that § 58.45 does not preclude holding of limited quantities of test or control article-feed mixtures for short periods of time in properly constructed and labeled containers in the animal rooms.

25. One comment objected to the proposed changes to § 58.47, arguing that it believed the current requirements respecting facilities for handling test and control articles have resulted in fewer mixups.

> Based on the comment, FDA has reconsidered the proposed revision of § 58.47. The agency agrees with the comment, in principle. Indeed, the agency intended the revision to be only editorial to simplify and to make clear that laboratories shall provide separate areas for receipt, mixing, and storage of test and control articles and their mixtures as necessary to prevent contamination or mixups. Inadvertently, however, the proposed revision would have deleted an essential requirement of good laboratory practice, i.e., the need to provide storage areas for test and control article mixtures

adequate to preserve the identity, strength, purity, and stability of the mixtures. For this reason, the agency has concluded that the regulation is appropriate as currently stated and existing § 58.47 is retained.

Maintenance and Calibration of Equipment

26. FDA proposed to revise § 58.63(b) to provide that written standard operating procedures respecting maintenance and calibration of equipment would allow laboratories to discard faulty equipment as an alternative to the current provisions of § 58.63(b), which provide only for the repair of equipment that fails or malfunctions. Under FDA's proposal, a testing facility would need to specify remedial action in the event of equipment failure or malfunction only when remedial action is "appropriate" to the particular piece of equipment. Three comments recommended that FDA amend § 58.63(a) to require testing, calibration, and/or standardization of equipment in accord with written standard operating procedures. The comments argued that by changing current § 58.63(a) in this fashion, FDA might delete § 58.63(b) in its entirety without substantively affecting the requirements of the GLP regulations applicable to laboratory equipment.

FDA advises that § 58.63(b) concerns not only setting forth in standard operating procedures the details of routine inspection, cleaning, maintenance, testing, calibration, and/or standardization of equipment, but it also concerns describing remedial actions to be taken when appropriate if the equipment fails or malfunctions. In promulgating existing § 58.63(b), FDA concluded that the specific features set forth in the regulations need to be included in equipment standard operating procedures because of the crucial role that properly used equipment plays in study conduct; a role which pervades every phase of a study and is vital to study quality and final report integrity. The comments did not provide any data that negate FDA's original determination. The agency continues to believe that specification of these features provides useful guidance to persons subject to the GLP regulations and concludes, therefore, that it would be inappropriate to delete § 58.63(b) from the regulations.

27. Section 58.63(b) requires in part that written standard operating procedures designate the person responsible for certain operations respecting equipment, i.e., routine inspection, cleaning, maintenance, testing, calibration, and/or standardization.

Although FDA did not propose to revise these requirements of § 58.63(b), three comments stated that by requiring that standard operating procedures designate an individual responsible for performing each operation, FDA obligates testing facilities to change their standard operating procedures frequently. The comments further argued that the requirement to make a copy of the standard operating procedures available to laboratory personnel is redundant to the requirements set forth in § 58.81(c) and should be deleted.

The comments misconstrue the meaning of the word "person" as it is used in § 58.63(b). The second sentence of § 58.63(b) requires, in pertinent part, that "the written standard operating procedures shall designate the person responsible for the performance of each operation * * *." As explained in paragraph 120 of the preamble to the final rule (43 FR 60001), FDA adopted the term "person" as defined in § 58.3(h) rather than the originally proposed term "individual" to allow the standard operating procedures to designate an organizational unit.

The agency agrees with the comment that § 58.63(b) is redundant to § 58.81(c) insofar as it provides for standard operating procedure availability. Accordingly, FDA is removing the phrase "and copies of the standard operating procedures shall be made available to laboratory personnel" from § 58.63(b).

28. Section 58.63(c) requires that a testing facility maintain written records of all equipment inspection, maintenance, testing, calibration, and/or standardizing operations. Two comments recommended that FDA delete § 58.63(c) in its entirety, arguing that if management is satisfied that the standard operating procedures are adequate, further requirements are unnecessary.

FDA does not agree with the comments. FDA carefully considered the necessity for maintaining the records specified in § 58.63(b) when the agency developed the current GLP regulations. FDA concluded that such records are necessary to reconstruct a study and to ensure the validity and integrity of the data that are obtained from a study (see paragraph 26 of this preamble and 43 FR 60001). The purpose of the record retention requirement is to provide documentation throughout the study of equipment function in accord with design specifications for the equipment, and equipment use in accord with standard operating procedures for maintenance and calibration of the equipment. FDA'S experience in administering the GLP regulations has shown the benefit of maintaining such records. For example, through FDA's laboratory inspection program, the agency has been able to identify the precise period of time of equipment malfunction by an examination of the equipment records. Thus, § 58.63(c) has made it possible to disregard the data collected by a single defective piece of equipment without having to disregard all the data obtained from a specific study.

Standard Operating Procedures

29. Two comments on the requirements for standard operating procedures suggested that § 58.81(a) be amended to permit appropriate supervisory personnel to authorize deviations from the written standard operating procedures, arguing that the study director may not have the technical expertise to evaluate such deviations. One of the comments further argued for the change on the ground that the principles of good laboratory practice established by the Organization for Economic Cooperation and Development of the World Health Organization do not require study director approval of all standard operating procedure deviations.

FDA does not accept the suggestion. As discussed in paragraph 9 of this preamble, it is not necessary for the study director to be technically competent in all aspects of a study to assure that appropriate action is taken in response to any circumstances that may affect the quality and integrity of a study. The study director, however, has to be aware of and authorize any deviations that could have an impact on the study. FDA does not agree that the responsibility of the study director, as set forth in § 58.81(a), is inconsistent with the Organization for Economic Cooperation and Development principles of GLP. Chapter 2, section 2.3 (Ref. 1, p. 27) of the Organization for Economic Cooperation and Development document defines the responsibilities of the study director, in part, as "ensur[ing] that the procedures specified in the study plan are followed, and that authorization for any modification is obtained and documented together with the reasons for them * * *." Accordingly, both the GLP regulations and the Organization for Economic Cooperation and Development principles of GLP require that the study director make certain that specified procedures are followed and that all modifications to the procedures in the approved study plan (i.e., standard operating procedures) are documented and approved.

30. One comment recommended that FDA amend § 58.81(b) to delete all examples of standard operating procedures that FDA requires a testing facility to establish on the ground that the list is not all-inclusive and may lead to misinterpretation.

> FDA disagrees with the recommendation. The examples listed in § 58.81(b) are those minimal laboratory procedures which the agency believes are essential to assuring the quality and integrity of the data generated in the course of any study (see 41 FR 51213). FDA recognizes that circumstances may necessitate establishment of additional standard operating procedures. The list is not intended to be all-inclusive and should not be interpreted as such.

31. Three comments objected to the proposed deletion of examples of laboratory manuals and standard operating procedures required to be in the laboratory under § 58.81(c). The comments argued that the listing of examples serves to spell out the agency's intent, helps laboratories decide which areas to cover, and that without such guidance a potential exists for misinterpretation of FDA's intent.

> FDA does not agree. Section 58.81(c) requires that each laboratory area have immediately available standard operating procedures relative to the laboratory procedures being performed. Unlike the list in § 58.81(b), which represents specific minimal requirements, the examples listed in § 58.81(c) encompass very broad areas. Each of the areas presented would require the preparation of a group of standard operating procedures to cover adequately the operations within that area. Consequently, the agency concludes that the list in § 58.81(c) is too broad to serve as useful guidance.

Reagents and Solutions

32. FDA received five comments that recommended that the agency amend § 58.83. Four comments stated that only those reagents and solutions used in the conduct of nonclinical laboratory studies need to be labeled in accord with the requirements of § 58.83, i.e.,

1987 Final Rule

"to indicate identity, titer or concentration, storage requirements, and expiration date" of the material. These comments argued that such a modification would allow the laboratory flexibility in designing the most suitable system to assure that deteriorated or outdated reagents and solutions are not used. The fifth comment recommended that FDA insert into the first sentence of § 58.83 the phrase "as appropriate" to make the provision read "all reagents and solutions in the laboratory areas shall be labeled to indicate identity, titer or concentration, storage requirements, and, as appropriate, expiration date." This comment argued that it was not necessary to have expiration dates on certain stable reagents and solutions such as water and saline.

FDA declines to amend § 58.83. The agency continues to believe, as discussed in paragraph 148 of the preamble to the final rule (43 FR 60003), that all reagents and solutions maintained in the laboratory area for use in the conduct of nonclinical laboratory studies should be labeled as required by § 58.83. Accordingly, the label should include the identity, titer or concentration, storage requirements, and expiration date. This label information is the minimum information necessary to make clear to the laboratory personnel that the reagents and solutions are suitable for use in the procedures specified in the protocol and to protect against inadvertent mixups of reagents and solutions that are used in nonclinical laboratory studies with those that are not intended for such use. Further, FDA disagrees with the comment that suggested that expiration dating is not necessary for some reagents and solutions. FDA believes that expiration dates should be required on all reagents and solutions, without regard to their stability so that there is no doubt about the suitability of the materials for use in nonclinical laboratory studies.

Animal Care

33. One comment recommended that FDA delete § 58.90(a) on the basis that requiring standard operating procedures for housing, feeding, handling, and care of animals is redundant to other provisions of the GLP regulations.

FDA recognizes that § 58.81(b)(2) requires testing facilities to establish standard operating procedures for animal care. Section 58.90(a), however, expressly specifies that standard operating procedures shall also cover animal housing, feeding, and handling. The agency believes that these items are essential features for providing adequate humane treatment of animals and, therefore, is retaining § 58.90(a).

34. Two comments objected to the proposed amendment of the requirements under §§ 58.90 (b) and (c) to provide that animals may be isolated rather than quarantined. The comments argued that allowing laboratories to develop isolation and health status evaluation procedures in lieu of quarantine may not provide adequate assurance of test animal health because such evaluations are done only on a small randomly selected number of animals and are not as reliable as an adequate quarantine period. One comment suggested that the term "segregated" or the term "separated" may more accurately reflect FDA's intent in amending §§ 58.90 (b) and (c) than does the term "isolated."

> As discussed in the preamble to the proposed amendments (49 FR 43533), substitution of a requirement for isolation and health status evaluations in lieu of quarantine of newly received animals will permit laboratories to develop specific isolation and health status evaluation procedures in concert with the age, species, and class of animals, and with the type of study to be done. As used in current § 58.90(b), the term "quarantine" connotes a rigid set of prestudy procedures which a facility is obligated to follow, including a mandatory holding period, specified diagnostic procedures, and the use of specialized facilities and animal care practices. The agency has concluded that isolation and health status evaluations should provide adequate precautions against entry of unhealthy animals into a study. Health status evaluations may be performed during the prestudy acclimation period. Under § 58.90(b), the health status of each animal is to be evaluated soon after receipt. Section 58.90(c) prohibits the entry of any diseased animal into the study.

> The agency has also concluded that a devoted area equipped to provide isolation of diseased animals is not necessary in all cases. As discussed in the preamble to the proposal (49 FR 43533), FDA believes that it should allow certain options for handling diseased animals, thereby permitting increased flexibility in laboratory operation. FDA agrees that the term "segregate" or the term "separate" rather than the term "isolate" could be used in as much as each term connotes "to set apart." Because "isolate" is a term commonly used and understood in contemporary veterinary medical practice,

1987 Final Rule

however, FDA will continue to use that term in these regulations.

35. One comment recommended that FDA amend § 58.90(d) to permit procedural means to provide "appropriate identification" of individual animals in a study.

FDA does not accept the recommendation. The agency notes that proper animal identification throughout a study is essential to study integrity. When animals are housed individually in cages, procedural means can be used to identify each individual animal, i.e., a cage card may be used if it provides all the information necessary to identify the animal specifically, and the animal handling standard operating procedures specify detailed procedures for preventing animal mixups. The agency is not aware, however, of any procedural means that could be used to identify adequately individual animals that are housed within a group in a cage. FDA advises that § 58.90(d) does not preclude identification by means other than the examples enumerated in that section provided that individual identification can be maintained and documented throughout a study.

Test and Control Article Characterization

36. One comment urged the agency to delete the requirement in § 58.105(b) for stability determination of test and control articles before initiation of the study. The comment argued that changing § 58.105(b) as recommended would make it consistent with FDA's proposed changes to § 58.105(a), which would allow test and control article characterization after completion of the study.

FDA disagrees with the recommendation. As discussed in the preamble to the proposal (49 FR 43533), FDA has concluded that characterization of test and control articles need not be performed until initial toxicology studies with the test article show reasonable promise of the article's reaching the marketplace. In arriving at this conclusion, the agency considered that prior knowledge of the precise molecular structure of a test article is not vital to the conduct of a valid toxicology test. It is important, however, to know the strength, purity, and stability of a test or control article that is used in a nonclinical laboratory study.

A stability determination of a test or control article conducted after completion of the nonclinical laboratory test with the article does not provide any information about the continued strength of either the test or control article previously given to the test system. Determining that the test and control articles are stable for the duration of the study is fundamental to interpreting the results of the study. For this reason, it would be inappropriate to allow for stability determinations only after-the-fact.

The agency does believe, however, that the continued strength of the test or control article may adequately be determined either by stability testing before initiation of the study or through appropriate periodic analysis of each batch. Section 58.105(b) currently allows stability testing of the test and control articles through periodic analysis only if it is not possible to determine their stability before study initiation. Because experience has shown that it is adequate either to determine stability of the test and control articles before initiation of a study or by periodic analysis of the articles while the study is in progress, the agency on its own initiative is revising § 58.105(b) to provide facilities and sponsors the flexibility to use either approach. Therefore, § 58.105(b) has been revised to provide for determination of the stability of the test or control article either before study initiation or through periodic analysis of each batch according to established standard operating procedures.

37. One comment observed that § 58.105(a) provides that testing facilities may rely on the labeling of marketed products for purposes of characterizing such products used as control articles in a study. The comment recommended that the agency also revise § 58.105(b) to allow product labeling to serve as documentation of stability for marketed products used as control articles.

> FDA declines to adopt this recommendation. The only stability information typically included on the labeling of marketed products is the expiration date. The manufacturer's expiration dating on a marketed product is not adequately precise to provide data on the strength of the control article used throughout a nonclinical laboratory study. Lacking precise stability information respecting the control article could raise doubts concerning whether the test and control articles are comparable. Furthermore, mixing the marketed product with a carrier or use of the product in a manner not

1987 Final Rule

in accord with its labeling could alter the stability characteristics of the product. For these reasons, FDA concludes that determination of the stability in accordance with the procedures in § 58.105(b) still is appropriate for any products used as control articles.

38. Several comments recommended that FDA revise § 58.105(c) to remove the current requirement that storage containers be assigned to a test article for the duration of a nonclinical laboratory study. The comments argued that the requirement is unnecessary and is inconsistent with the Organization for Economic Cooperation and Development principles of GLP. One comment alleged that the statement is vague and questioned whether the provision would permit a storage container that a laboratory emptied during the conduct of, but before completion of, a study to be destroyed or reused. The same comment also questioned whether, as the test article is depleted during the conduct of a study, the provision would permit a laboratory to transfer the test article into a container smaller than that originally assigned to the article.

> FDA does not believe that it would be appropriate to eliminate the storage container provision in § 58.105(c). FDA advises that the provision simply requires that each test article storage container be assigned to a test article at the beginning of a study and remain so assigned until the study is completed, terminated, or discontinued. The test article may not be transferred to different sized storage containers as a study progresses, nor may assigned storage containers be destroyed while a study is in progress.

> The agency recognizes that it may be inconvenient for laboratories, especially small laboratories, to devote space to a test article container which is emptied before a study is completely terminated, or discontinued, or which might be replaced by progressively smaller containers while a study is in progress. Destroying or reusing or otherwise substituting for originally assigned, identified test article storage containers, however, could adversely affect the integrity of the study. FDA established the current provision because the agency observed a lack of accountability for test materials, ostensibly due to the very acts proscribed by the regulation, i.e., transfer of test articles to different sized containers and destruction of empty containers during the progress of nonclinical laboratory studies.

FDA continues to believe that the requirement concerning assignment of storage containers is necessary to ensure the integrity of a study. For example, the mere act of transferring a test article from one storage container to another introduces the opportunity for contamination of the test article by other laboratory materials or for mix-ups with other laboratory materials. In addition, during a transfer the test article would be exposed to air-borne contaminants as well as to moisture, either of which may compromise the integrity of the test article.

FDA also believes that requiring that containers be assigned to a test article for the duration of a study is fully consistent with the Organization for Economic Cooperation and Development principles of GLP. Chapter 2, section 2.3 (Ref. 1, p. 31) of the Organization for Economic Cooperation and Development document states that "storage container(s) should carry identification information, earliest expiration date, and specific storage instructions." Although the Organization for Economic Cooperation and Development document does not further characterize storage instructions that the Organization for Economic Cooperation and Development would recommend be included on containers, FDA concludes that its regulation identifies a "specific" storage instruction that is necessary to assure the integrity of the test article.

Mixtures of Articles with Carriers

39. Two comments argued that the requirements in § 58.113(a) to determine the uniformity, concentration, and stability of test and control articles in mixtures is unnecessarily burdensome for short-term studies. One comment stated that such tests are not necessary for test articles that are prepared and dispensed on the same day as used in single-dose acute toxicity tests. The comments suggested that the agency revise § 58.113(a) to require that tests of mixtures of test and control articles need be conducted only "for studies other than short-term."

Section 58.113(a) requires, for all test or control articles mixed with a carrier, a determination of the uniformity of the mixture and a periodic analysis of the concentration of the test or control article in the mixture. In addition, § 58.113(a)(2), as amended, requires a determination of the stability of the test or control article in the mixture adequate

1987 Final Rule

to support time of use. Each of these analyses is necessary to assure that the test system is exposed to the test or to the control article in the amounts specifically designated in the protocol for a study. Determination of the uniformity of a mixture assures that each member of the test system receives the intended dose of test or control article. Periodic analysis of the concentration of the test or control article serves as a spot check to assure that the test or control article mixture has been prepared properly and in accord with the protocol and with applicable standard operating procedures. Determining the stability of the test or control article in the mixture helps to determine the period of time during which the test or control article mixture may be suitable for administration to the test system. FDA believes that knowledge of the dose of test or control article used in any test is essential for the proper evaluation of the results of that test. For these reasons, FDA has concluded that the requirements of § 58.113(a) should continue to apply to short-term tests as well as to studies other than short term.

As discussed in paragraph 36 of this preamble, however, FDA has decided to allow facilities and sponsors the flexibility to determine the stability of test and control articles either before study initiation or through periodic analysis of each batch according to established standard operating procedures. The agency believes that it is appropriate to allow similar flexibility with respect to determining the stability of mixtures of articles with carriers. For this reason, on its own initiative, FDA has revised § 58.113(a)(2) to allow determination of the stability of test and control articles in the mixture either before study initiation or through periodic analysis of the mixture according to established standard operating procedures.

40. One comment recommended that FDA delete § 58.113(a)(1), alleging that periodic determinations of the test or control article in mixtures is routine and provisions respecting such determination would more appropriately be included in § 58.35(b)(3).

The comment misconstrues the function of the QAU (see especially paragraphs 12 and 18 of this preamble). Current § 58.35(b)(3), as well as § 58.35(b)(3) as revised by this final rule assigns responsibility for periodic inspection of laboratory operations to the QAU. The QAU does not, indeed, under §

58.35(a), the QAU may not conduct any portion of a study. Rather, it is responsible for assuring that a study is conducted according to the protocol, the standard operating procedures, and the GLP regulations.

Protocol

41. A comment urged the agency to delete the provision in current § 58.120(a)(14) (final § 58.120(a)(10)) that requires that the protocol for each study identify the records for the study to be maintained. The comment argued that the requirement in renumbered § 58.120(a)(10) is redundant to the same requirements in §§ 58.33(f), 58.190(a), and 58.195(b).

   FDA recognizes that §§ 58.33(f), 58.190(a), and 58.195(b) address records that the GLP regulations require a testing facility to retain in all events. As the authorized master plan for a study, however, the protocol should identify all records of the study to be maintained by the testing facility to inform all study participants fully of recordkeeping obligations. The agency believes that inclusion of this information in the protocol is essential to ensure adequate documentation of the conduct of the study.

   For these reasons, FDA declines to remove § 58.120(a)(10) from the GLP regulations.

42. One comment recommended that FDA delete the provision in current § 58.120(a)(16) (final § 58.120(a)(12)) that requires that the protocol for each study include a statement of the proposed statistical methods to be used in the study. The comment argued that a determination of the statistical methods used to evaluate data can, in many cases, be made only after data have been reviewed.

   FDA recognizes that circumstances occasionally require a testing facility to modify the proposed statistical methods for analysis of the data in a given study. Good scientific practice, however, requires consideration of the statistical analysis of a study as part of the design of the study to assess whether the objectives of the study can be met. FDA concludes that the requirement is appropriate.

Conduct of a Nonclinical Laboratory Study

43. Section 58.130(c) provides that materials derived from a test system for examination or analysis (specimens) are to be identified by test system, study, nature, and the date of collection, and requires that such identification is to be located on the specimen container or is to accompany the specimen in a manner that precludes error in the recording and storage of data. Five comments argued that the requirements under § 58.130(c) for specimen identification are overly restrictive and suggested that management should be responsible for determining methods for identifying specimens.

> The identification requirements specified in § 58.130(c) are designed to preclude error during the conduct of a nonclinical laboratory study. FDA has reviewed the requirements and has concluded that the identifying information specified in the regulation is the minimum information needed to distinguish each specimen from all others that have been collected in the facility thereby protecting against mixups and permitting orderly storage of specimens. Such information also shows whether the data collected on each specimen are assigned to the correct component of the test system.

> FDA has always provided flexibility in the methods to be used for identifying the specimens in that the identifying information can be encoded through, for example, the use of accession numbers affixed to the specimen with the numbers decoded in accompanying information (see, e.g., paragraph 205 of the preamble to the final rule (43 FR 60008)). The agency believes that the requirements with respect to specimen identification are the minimum requirements necessary to prevent mixup of specimens or lost specimen identity.

44. Two comments disagreed with FDA's proposal to revise § 58.130(d), which currently requires that records of gross findings for a specimen from postmortem (necropsy) observations shall, in all cases, be provided to a pathologist during study of the specimen. The proposed revision provides only that such records "should" be made available to the pathologist. Four comments supported the proposed change on the ground that the resulting flexibility allows "blinding" of the pathologist. One comment suggested that § 58.130(d) be deleted in its entirety or,

alternatively, modified by specifying that the records are to be provided to the pathologist "if required by the protocol."

> FDA established § 58.130(d) in the belief that the provision would increase the pathologist's ability to describe correctly microscopic findings and to relate such findings properly with the gross postmortem observations (41 FR 51214). FDA continues to believe that for most studies it is important for the pathologist to have available the records of gross findings when examining a specimen histopathologically. The agency recognizes, however, that for certain nonclinical laboratory studies it may be appropriate for pathologists to evaluate the histopathological specimens without being informed of the necropsy findings. The change made in the regulation will permit the study director, in concert with management, to determine the need for "blinding" in relation to the specific objectives of the study.

> FDA advises that it continues to believe that for most studies it is a preferred practice not to use "blinding" in histopathological evaluation. For this reason, the agency is not deleting § 58.130(d) as suggested by one comment. The alternative phrase "if required by the protocol" suggested by the comment would serve the same purpose as the modification proposed by the agency. Therefore, the agency is adopting § 58.130(d) as proposed.

45. One comment on § 58.130(e) requested that FDA clarify the meaning of the term "automated data collection systems," stating that it is unclear whether § 58.130(e) applies to tabulation of source data from "hard" copy by automated systems.

> As discussed in paragraph 7a. of this preamble, hand-recorded data collected during a study are "raw data." The subsequent entry of these hand-recorded data into a computer system, for example, by data processing clerks or through the use of optical readers, does not alter the status of the hand-recorded data as "raw data." The processing of these data by the computer, e.g., tabulation, is not "direct data input" and is, therefore, not encompassed by the requirements of § 58.130(e).

1987 Final Rule

Reporting of Nonclinical Laboratory Study Results

46. Section 58.185(a) requires that a final report be prepared for each nonclinical laboratory study conducted and specifies the minimum information that shall be included in a final report. One comment urged that § 58.185(a) should be modified to require final reports to include the specified information only "where appropriate" to make the requirements respecting final reports consistent with FDA's proposal to change § 58.120(a) respecting protocols. Alternatively, the comment urged that, at the least, § 58.185(a)(8), which requires that any final report shall include a description of the dosage, dosage regimen, route of administration, and duration, should be so modified. The comment argued that some of the information required under this paragraph is not applicable to certain studies involving medical devices.

> FDA proposed to change § 58.120(a) in recognition of the fact that certain of the enumerated items are not necessary for the protocols for all studies. FDA has carefully reviewed each of the items listed in § 58.185(a) and has concluded that the information required by this section to be included in a final report for a nonclinical laboratory study is necessary to evaluate any such study. FDA notes that § 58.185 currently allows certain appropriate flexibilities where specified information is determined by the laboratory not to be relevant to a study. For example, § 58.185(a)(4) provides that test and control articles may be identified by "other appropriate characteristics" and § 58.185(a)(7) includes the term "where applicable." The agency believes that the information required by § 58.185(a)(8) is applicable to studies involving medical devices. For example, "dosage" and "dosage regimen" for devices may be expressed in units used per animal at a designated frequency of use. "Route of administration" may describe the means by which the device is used in relation to the animal. "Duration" would pertain to the period of time the device was tested in the animal. These clarifications should permit nonclinical laboratory studies on medical devices to be reported properly.

47. Section 58.185(a)(10) requires that each final report of a nonclinical laboratory study include the name of the study director, the names of other scientists or professionals, and the names of all supervisory personnel involved in the study. One comment recommended that FDA revise § 58.185(a)(10) to

require identification only of the study director and of the principal scientists involved in the study.

> FDA disagrees with this suggestion. Supervisors play an important role in the data collection process. They supervise those who perform the procedures, may recommend or actually provide training, and assure that data collection is carried out in accordance with the protocol, the standard operating procedures, and the GLP regulations. The names of all scientists, professionals, and supervisors are needed to assure the accountability of all of those individuals responsible for the integrity of the study. The comment did not provide any data or information to support its recommendation to revise § 58.185(a)(10) and the agency concludes that it should retain the current requirement.

48a. Section 58.185(a)(12) requires that the final report of a nonclinical laboratory study include the signed and dated reports of each of the individual scientists or other professionals who were involved in the study. Two comments recommended that FDA revise § 58.185(a)(12) to allow for combined reports signed by the principal scientists. According to the comments, allowing for such combined reports would be consistent with the Organization for Economic Cooperation and Development principles of GLP.

> The agency does not believe that a combined report from scientists of different disciplines would be appropriate. Each individual scientist involved in a study has to be accountable for reporting data, information, and views within his or her designated area of responsibility. Reports which combine the data, information, and views of more than one such person would obscure the individual's accountability for accurate reporting. Furthermore, FDA believes that the comment has misinterpreted the standard that the Organization for Economic Cooperation and Development established respecting reports of persons involved in a nonclinical laboratory study. Chapter 2, section 2.3 (Ref. 1, p. 36) of the Organization for Economic Cooperation and Development document provides that "if reports of principal scientists from co-operating disciplines are included in the final report, they should sign and date them." It provides further that the final report should contain the "names of other principal personnel having contributed reports to the final report." These provisions do not imply that combined reports would

1987 Final Rule

be appropriate. Rather, they support the need for individual accountability. The Organization for Economic Cooperation and Development provisions are entirely consistent with the provisions of § 58.185(a)(12).

48b. On its own initiative, FDA is amending § 58.185(b) to provide that the final report shall contain the dated signature of the study director to conform the provision to the definition of "study completion date" being added by this final rule (see paragraph 6 of this preamble).

Storage and Retrieval of Records and Data

49. FDA proposed to revise § 58.190(a) to allow wet specimens and specimens from mutagenicity tests to be discarded after evaluation and recording. The agency's proposal was supported by several comments. One comment, however, requested that the agency clarify the meaning of "mutagenicity tests" as the term is used in § 58.190(a). The comment asked whether, for example, in vitro cell transformation is interpreted to be a mutagenicity test under this provision.

> FDA advises that, for the purpose of § 58.190(a), the agency considers mutagenicity tests to be those tests designed to assess the capacity of a test or control article to induce heritable changes in a test system. Accordingly, FDA considers in vitro cell transformation to be a mutagenicity test as the term is used in the GLP regulations.

50. One comment recommended that FDA further revise § 58.190(a) to assure that the regulation makes clear that final reports must be retained.

> As discussed at length in the preamble to the proposal (49 FR 43534), FDA intended to exclude from the retention requirements of the GLP regulations specimens that are relatively fragile or contribute only in a minor way to safety evaluation. FDA did not intend to change the current requirement that final reports of any nonclinical laboratory study are to be retained in accordance with § 58.195. To preclude any possible confusion regarding the requirement that final reports must be retained, FDA is rewording § 58.190(a) to read "all raw data, documentation, protocols, final reports, and specimens (except those specimens obtained from mutagenicity tests and wet specimens of

blood, urine, feces, and biological fluids) generated as a result of a nonclinical laboratory study shall be retained."

Retention of Records

51. FDA proposed to delete from current § 58.195(c) the listed examples of materials that the agency believes need to be retained only so long as the quality of the preparation affords evaluation. One comment noted that § 58.195(c) should be further revised to delete wet specimens to be consistent with the proposed revisions in § 58.190(a) (see paragraph 50 of this preamble).

> FDA agrees with the comment and in this final rule is conforming § 58.195(c) to revised § 58.190(a). In pertinent part, § 58.195(c) now reads "Wet specimens (except those specimens obtained from mutagenicity tests and wet specimens of blood, urine, feces, and biological fluids), samples of test or control articles, and specially prepared material * * *."

52. Two comments suggested that FDA should specifically provide in new § 58.195(g) that records to be retained under the GLP regulations may be retained as magnetic media.

> Section 58.195(g), which is being added to Part 58 by this final rule, provides that records respecting a nonclinical laboratory study may be retained as original records or as true copies such as photocopies, microfilm, microfiche, or other accurate reproductions of the original records. Magnetic media could qualify as either "original records" or "accurate reproductions of the original records." This conclusion is consistent with § 58.3(k), which includes "magnetic media" within the meaning of "raw data." Consequently, the agency does not believe that it is necessary to change new § 58.195(g) in order to achieve the result desired by the comments.

Reference

The following reference has been placed on display in the Dockets Management Branch (HFA-305), Food and Drug Administration, Rm. 4-62, 5600 Fishers Lane, Rockville, MD 20857, and may be seen in that office between 9 a.m. and 4 p.m., Monday through Friday.

1987 Final Rule

1. "Good Laboratory Practice in the Testing of Chemicals," Organization for Economic Cooperation and Development Publications, Paris, France, 1982.

Economic Assessment

As announced in the proposal, FDA has examined the economic consequences of this final rule in accordance with Executive Order 12291 and the Regulatory Flexibility Act (Pub. L. 96-354). At that time, the agency concluded that the changes would not constitute a major rule as defined in the Order and that no regulatory flexibility analysis would be required. The agency also certified that the revisions would not have a significant impact on a substantial number of small entities. The agency has not received any new information or comments that would alter its previous determination.

Environmental Impact

The agency has determined under 21 CFR 25.24(a)(10) that this action is of a type that does not individually or cumulatively have a significant effect on the human environment. Therefore, neither an environmental assessment nor an environmental impact statement is required.

Paperwork Reduction Act of 1980

Sections 58.35(b) (1), (3), and (6), 58.63(b), 58.90(c), 58.105(a), 58.120(a), 58.130(e), and 58.190 (a) and (e) of this final rule contain collection of information requirements. FDA submitted a copy of the proposed rule containing the same requirements to the Office of Management and Budget (OMB). These collection of information requirements were approved under OMB Control No. 0910-0203.

List of Subjects in 21 CFR Part 58

Laboratories.

Therefore, under the Federal Food, Drug, and Cosmetic Act and under 21 CFR 5.11, Part 58 is amended as follows:

Part 58 -- Good Laboratory Practice for Nonclinical Laboratory Studies

1. The authority citation for 21 CFR Part 58 is revised to read as follows:

Authority: Secs. 306, 402(a), 406, 408, 409, 502, 503, 505, 506, 507, 510, 512-516, 518-520, 701(a), 706, 801, Pub. L. 717, 52 Stat. 1045-1046 as amended, 1049-1053 as amended, 1055, 1058 as amended, 55 Stat. 851 as amended, 59 Stat. 463 as amended, 68 Stat. 511-517 as amended, 72 Stat. 1785-1788 as amended, 76 Stat. 794 as amended, 82 Stat. 343-351, 90 Stat. 539-574 (21 U.S.C. 336, 342(a), 346, 346a, 348, 352, 353, 355, 356, 357, 360, 360b-360f, 360f, 360h-360j, 371(a), 376, 381); secs. 215, 351, 354-360F, Pub. L. 410, 58 Stat. 690, 702 as amended, 82 Stat. 1173-1186 as amended (42 U.S.C. 216, 262, 263b-263n); 21 CFR 5.11.

2. In § 58.1 by designating the existing text as paragraph (a) and adding new paragraph (b), to read as follows:

    § 58.1 Scope.

    * * * * *

    (b) References in this part to regulatory sections of the Code of Federal Regulations are to Chapter I of Title 21, unless otherwise noted.

3. In § 58.3 by removing the phrase "of this chapter" wherever it appears; by revising paragraphs (c), (d), and (e)(8); by removing and reserving paragraph (e)(12); by replacing "in section 513 of the act" with "in Part 860" in paragraph (e)(17); by replacing "section 514 of the act" with "in Part 861" in paragraph (e)(18); and by adding new paragraphs (o) and (p), to read as follows:

    § 58.3 Definitions.

    * * * * *

    (c) "Control article" means any food additive, color additive, drug, biological product, electronic product, medical device for human use, or any article other than a test article, feed, or water that is administered to the test system in the course of a nonclinical laboratory study for the purpose of establishing a basis for comparison with the test article.

    (d) "Nonclinical laboratory study" means in vivo or in vitro experiments in which test articles are studied prospectively in test systems under laboratory conditions to determine their safety. The term does not include studies utilizing human subjects or clinical studies or field trials in animals. The term does not include basic exploratory studies carried out to determine whether a test article has any potential utility or to determine physical or chemical characteristics of a test article.

    (e) * * *

(8) Data and information about a substance submitted as part of the procedures for establishing a tolerance for unavoidable contaminants in food and food-packaging materials, described in Parts 109 and 509.

* * * * *

(12) [Reserved]

* * * * *

(o) "Study initiation date" means the date the protocol is signed by the study director.

(p) "Study completion date" means the date the final report is signed by the study director.

4. In § 58.31 by revising paragraph (b), to read as follows:

§ 58.31 Testing facility management.

* * * * *

(b) Replace the study director promptly if it becomes necessary to do so during the conduct of a study.

* * * * *

5. In § 58.35 by removing paragraph (e), by revising paragraphs (a) and (b) introductory text, (1) and (3), and by adding an OMB number at the end of the section to read as follows:

§ 58.35 Quality assurance unit.

(a) A testing facility shall have a quality assurance unit which shall be responsible for monitoring each study to assure management that the facilities, equipment, personnel, methods, practices, records, and controls are in conformance with the regulations in this part. For any given study, the quality assurance unit shall be entirely separate from and independent of the personnel engaged in the direction and conduct of that study.

(b) The quality assurance unit shall: (1) Maintain a copy of a master schedule sheet of all nonclinical laboratory studies conducted at the testing facility indexed by test article and containing the test system, nature of study, date study was initiated, current status of each study, identity of the sponsor, and name of the study director.

* * * * *

(3) Inspect each nonclinical laboratory study at intervals adequate to assure the integrity of the study and maintain written and properly signed records of each periodic inspection showing the date of the inspection, the study inspected, the phase or segment of the study inspected, the person performing the inspection, findings and problems, action recommended and taken to resolve existing problems, and any scheduled date for reinspection. Any problems found during the course of an inspection which are likely to affect study integrity shall be brought to the attention of the study director and management immediately.

* * * * *

(Collection of information requirements approved by the Office of Management and Budget under number 0910-0203.)

6. By revising § 58.41, to read as follows:

§ 58.41 General.

Each testing facility shall be of suitable size and construction to facilitate the proper conduct of nonclinical laboratory studies. It shall be designed so that there is a degree of separation that will prevent any function or activity from having an adverse effect on the study.

7. In § 58.43 by removing paragraph (e) and by revising the first sentence of paragraph (c) to read as follows:

§ 58.43 Animal care facilities.

* * * * *

(c) Separate areas shall be provided, as appropriate, for the diagnosis, treatment, and control of laboratory animal diseases. * * *

* * * * *

8. In § 58.45 by revising the last sentence, to read as follows:

§ 58.45 Animal supply facilities.

* * * Perishable supplies shall be preserved by appropriate means.

1987 Final Rule

9. By revising § 58.49, to read as follows:

§ 58.49 Laboratory operation areas.

Separate laboratory space shall be provided, as needed, for the performance of the routine and specialized procedures required by nonclinical laboratory studies.

§ 58.53 [Removed]

10. By removing § 58.53 Administrative and personnel facilities.

11. By revising § 58.61, to read as follows:

§ 58.61 Equipment design.

Equipment used in the generation, measurement, or assessment of data and equipment used for facility environmental control shall be of appropriate design and adequate capacity to function according to the protocol and shall be suitably located for operation, inspection, cleaning, and maintenance.

12. In § 58.63 by revising paragraph (b) and by adding an OMB numbert at the end of the section, to read as follows:

§ 58.63 Maintenance and calibration of equipment.

* * * * *

(b) The written standard operating procedures required under § 58.81(b)(11) shall set forth in sufficient detail the methods, materials, and schedules to be used in the routine inspection, cleaning, maintenance, testing, calibration, and/or standardization of equipment, and shall specify, when appropriate, remedial action to be taken in the event of failure or malfunction of equipment. The written standard operating procedures shall designate the person responsible for the performance of each operation.

* * * * *

(Collection of information requirements approved by the Office of Management and Budget under number 0910-0203.)

13. In § 58.81 by revising the first sentence of paragraph (c), to read as follows:

§ 58.81 Standard operating procedures.

* * * * *

(c)   Each laboratory area shall have immediately available laboratory manuals and standard operating procedures relative to the laboratory procedures being performed. * * *

* * * * *

14. In § 58.90 by revising paragraphs (b) and (c) and by adding an OMB number at the end of the section, to read as follows:

§ 58.90 Animal care.

* * * * *

(b)   All newly received animals from outside sources shall be isolated and their health status shall be evaluated in accordance with acceptable veterinary medical practice.

(c)   At the initiation of a nonclinical laboratory study, animals shall be free of any disease or condition that might interfere with the purpose or conduct of the study. If, during the course of the study, the animals contract such a disease or condition, the diseased animals shall be isolated, if necessary. These animals may be treated for disease or signs of disease provided that such treatment does not interfere with the study. The diagnosis, authorizations of treatment, description of treatment, and each date of treatment shall be documented and shall be retained.

* * * * *

(Collection of information requirements approved by the Office of Management and Budget under number 0910-0203.)

15. In § 58.105 by revising the first sentence of paragraph (a), by revising paragraph (b), and by adding an OMB number at the end of the section, to read as follows:

§ 58.105 Test and control article characterization.

(a)   The identity, strength, purity, and composition or other characteristics which will appropriately define the test or

1987 Final Rule

control article shall be determined for each batch and shall be documented. * * *

(b) The stability of each test or control article shall be determined by the testing facility or by the sponsor either: (1) Before study initiation, or (2) concomitantly according to written standard operating procedures, which provide for periodic analysis of each batch.

* * * * *

(Collection of information requirements approved by the Office of Management and Budget under number 0910-0203.)

16. In § 58.113 by revising paragraph (a)(2), to read as follows:

§ 58.113 Mixtures of articles with carriers.

(a)   * * *

(2) To determine the stability of the test and control articles in the mixture as required by the conditions of the study either (i) before study initiation, or (ii) concomitantly according to written standard operating procedures which provide for periodic analysis of the test and control articles in the mixture.

* * * * *

17. In § 58.120 by revising paragraph (a) and by adding an OMB number at the end of the section, to read as follows:

§ 58.120 Protocol.

(a) Each study shall have an approved written protocol that clearly indicates the objectives and all methods for the conduct of the study. The protocol shall contain, as applicable, the following information:

(1) A descriptive title and statement of the purpose of the study.

(2) Identification of the test and control articles by name, chemical abstract number, or code number.

(3) The name of the sponsor and the name and address of the testing facility at which the study is being conducted.

(4) The number, body weight range, sex, source of supply, species, strain, substrain, and age of the test system.

(5) The procedure for identification of the test system.

(6) A description of the experimental design, including the methods for the control of bias.

(7) A description and/or identification of the diet used in the study as well as solvents, emulsifiers, and/or other materials used to solubilize or suspend the test or control articles before mixing with the carrier. The description shall include specifications for acceptable levels of contaminants that are reasonably expected to be present in the dietary materials and are known to be capable of interfering with the purpose or conduct of the study if present at levels greater than established by the specifications.

(8) Each dosage level, expressed in milligrams per kilogram of body weight or other appropriate units, of the test or control article to be administered and the method and frequency of administration.

(9) The type and frequency of tests, analyses, and measurements to be made.

(10) The records to be maintained.

(11) The date of approval of the protocol by the sponsor and the dated signature of the study director.

(12) A statement of the proposed statistical methods to be used.

* * * * *

(Collection of information requirements approved by the Office of Management and Budget under number 0910-0203.)

18. In § 58.130 by revising paragraphs (d) and (e) and by adding an OMB number at the end of the section, to read as follows:

§ 58.130 Conduct of a nonclinical laboratory study.

* * * * *

1987 Final Rule

(d) Records of gross findings for a specimen from postmortem observations should be available to a pathologist when examining that specimen histopathologically.

(e) All data generated during the conduct of a nonclinical laboratory study, except those that are generated by automated data collection systems, shall be recorded directly, promptly, and legibly in ink. All data entries shall be dated on the date of entry and signed or initialed by the person entering the data. Any change in entries shall be made so as not to obscure the original entry, shall indicate the reason for such change, and shall be dated and signed or identified at the time of the change. In automated data collection systems, the individual responsible for direct data input shall be identified at the time of data input. Any change in automated data entries shall be made so as not to obscure the original entry, shall indicate the reason for change, shall be dated, and the responsible individual shall be identified.

(Collection of information requirements approved by the Office of Management and Budget under number 0910-0203.)

19. In § 58.185 by revising paragraph (b), to read as follows:

§ 58.185 Reporting of nonclinical laboratory study results.

* * * * *

(b) The final report shall be signed and dated by the study director.

20. In § 58.190 by revising paragraphs (a) and (e) and by adding an OMB number at the end of the section, to read as follows:

§ 58.190 Storage and retrieval of records and data.

(a) All raw data, documentation, protocols, final reports, and specimens (except those specimens obtained from mutagenicity tests and wet specimens of blood, urine, feces, and biological fluids) generated as a result of a nonclinical laboratory study shall be retained.

* * * * *

(e) Material retained or referred to in the archives shall be indexed to permit expedient retrieval.

(Collection of information requirements approved by the Office of Management and Budget under number 0910-0203.)

21. In § 58.195 by revising paragraph (c), redesignating paragraph (g) as paragraph (h), and adding new paragraph (g), to read as follows:

§ 58.195 Retention of records.

* * * * *

(c)   Wet specimens (except those specimens obtained from mutagenicity tests and wet specimens of blood, urine, feces, and biological fluids), samples of test or control articles, and specially prepared material, which are relatively fragile and differ markedly in stability and quality during storage, shall be retained only as long as the quality of the preparation affords evaluation. In no case shall retention be required for longer periods than those set forth in paragraphs (a) and (b) of this section.

* * * * *

(g)   Records required by this part may be retained either as original records or as true copies such as photocopies, microfilm, microfiche, or other accurate reproductions of the original records.

* * * * *

§ 58.204 [Amended]

22. In § 58.204 Notice of and opportunity for hearing on proposed disqualification in paragraph (b) by removing "of this chapter."

§ 58.213 [Amended]

23. In § 58.213 Public disclosure of information regarding disqualification in paragraph (b) by removing "of this chapter."

§ 58.219 [Amended]

24. In § 58.219 Reinstatement of a disqualified testing facility by removing "of this chapter."

[FR Doc. 87-20375 Filed 9-3-87; 8:45 am]

Part II

Guidance Documents

Bioresearch Monitoring Good Laboratory Practice

Bioresearch Monitoring Good Laboratory Practice[1]

Compliance Program 7348.808

(Nonclinical Laboratories)

Date of Issuance: February 21, 2001

Guidance for FDA Staff

Food and Drug Administration
Compliance Program Guidance Manual

Chapter 48
Bioresearch Monitoring

This document is intended to provide guidance. It represents the Agency's current thinking on this topic. It does not create or confer any rights for or on any person and does not operate to bind Food and Drug Administration (FDA) or the public. An alternative approach may be used if such approach satisfies the requirements of the applicable statute and regulations.

Cover Page	
Part I	Background
Part II	Implementation
Part III	Inspectional
Part IV	Analytical
Part V	Regulatory/Administrative
Part VI	References and Program Contact
Part VII	Headquarters' Responsibilities
Attachment A	Computer Systems

---

[1] Available on the FDA website at: http://www.fda.gov/ICECI/
EnforcementActions/BioresearchMonitoring/ucm133789.htm

Compliance Program Guidance Manual Cover Page

Data Reporting	
Product Codes	**Product/Assignment Codes**
51Z OR 52Z	04808 Chemical Contaminants (EPA)
45Z, 46Z	09808 Food Additives
57Z, 99Z	41808 Biologics (Therapeutics) 42808 Biologics (Blood) 45808 Biologics (Vaccines)
60Z, 61Z	48808 Human Drugs
68Z, 69Z	68808 Animal Drugs
73Z, 74Z 94Z OR 95Z	83808 Medical and Radiological Devices

Field Reporting Requirements

All establishment inspection reports (EIRs), complete with attachments, exhibits, and any post-inspectional correspondence are to be submitted promptly to the assigning Center. If an EIR contains serious findings raising the possibility of one or more violations of the Federal Food Drug & Cosmetic Act (FFDCA) or other Federal statutes, a copy of the EIR should be forwarded to the District Compliance Branch at the time it is sent to the Center. If an FDA-483 is issued, a copy will be faxed to the Center contact identified in the assignment.

If the district becomes aware of any significant adverse inspectional, analytical, or other information which may affect the agency's new product approval decisions with respect to a firm, the district should immediately notify the responsible Center program office via electronic mail, fax, or by phone.

If samples are collected for analysis, the analyzing laboratory will submit copies of the Collection Report and the Analytical Work sheets to the District Office and the assigning Center.

Part I – Background

The FFDCA and Public Health Service Act require that sponsors of FDA-regulated products submit evidence of their product's safety in research and/or marketing applications. These products include food and color additives, animal drugs, human drugs and biological products, human medical devices, diagnostic products, and electronic products. FDA uses these data to answer questions regarding:

- The toxicity profile of the article.

- The observed no adverse effect dose level in the test system.

- The risks associated with clinical studies involving humans or animals.

- The potential teratogenic, carcinogenic, or other adverse effects of the article.

- The level of use that can be approved.

The importance of nonclinical laboratory studies to FDA's public health decisions demands that they be conducted according to scientifically sound protocols and with meticulous attention to quality.

In the 1970s, FDA inspections of nonclinical laboratories revealed that some studies submitted in support of the safety of regulated products had not been conducted in accord with acceptable practice, and that accordingly data from such studies was not always of the quality and integrity to assure product safety. As a result of these findings, FDA promulgated the Good Laboratory Practice (GLP) Regulations, 21 CFR Part 58, on December 22, 1978 (43 FR 59986). The regulations became effective June 1979. The regulations establish standards for the conduct and reporting of nonclinical laboratory studies and are intended to assure the quality and integrity of safety data submitted to FDA.

FDA relies on documented adherence to GLP requirements by nonclinical laboratories in judging the acceptability of safety data submitted in support of research and/or marketing permits. FDA has implemented this program of regular inspections and data audits to monitor laboratory compliance with the GLP requirements.

Part II - Implementation

A. Objective

1. To verify the quality and integrity of data submitted in a research or marketing application.

2. To inspect (approximately every two years) nonclinical laboratories conducting safety studies that are intended to support applications for research or marketing of regulated products.

3. To audit safety studies and determine the degree of compliance with GLP regulations.

B. Program Management Instructions

This program provides for the inspection of public, private, and government nonclinical laboratories that perform testing on food and color additives, animal drugs, human drugs and biological products, human medical devices, diagnostic, and electronic products.

Assignments for the initial GLP inspection of a specific university department or government facility are to be initiated only after the facility has been informed of the agency's intent to inspect by a letter from the Bioresearch Monitoring Program Coordinator (HFC-230). Notification of subsequent inspections of these laboratory facilities is not necessary.

Consulting laboratories, contractors, and grantees are covered by the GLPs to the degree that they provide data for a nonclinical laboratory study. The sponsor or person contracting the service must notify them that the service is part of a nonclinical laboratory study that must be conducted in compliance with the provisions of this part. The consulting laboratory, contractor, or grantee

Is only required to comply with those parts of the GLPs that are appropriate to the nature of their contributions to a study.

FDA Centers or ORA headquarters will initiate all nonclinical laboratory inspections.

C. Types of Inspections

1.Surveillance Inspections

Surveillance inspections are periodic, routine determinations of a laboratory's compliance with GLP regulations. These inspections include a facility inspection and audits of on-going and/or recently completed studies.

2. Directed Inspections

Directed inspections are assigned to achieve a specific purpose, such as:

a. Verifying the reliability, integrity, and compliance of critical safety studies being reviewed in support of pending applications.

b. Investigating issues involving potentially unreliable safety data and/or violative conditions brought to FDA's attention.

c. Re-inspecting laboratories previously classified OAI (usually within 6 months after the firm responds to a Warning Letter).

d. Verifying the results from third party audits or sponsor audits submitted to FDA for consideration in determining whether to accept or reject questionable or suspect studies.

D. Inspection Teams (FDA Personnel)

Team inspections may be conducted.

1. Team Leader

A field investigator will serve as team leader and is responsible for the cooperative conduct of the inspection. Responsibilities of the team leader are explained in the Investigations Operations Manual (IOM) 502.4.

2. Field Analyst/Headquarters Participant

Field analyst or headquarters participant will serve as scientific or technical support to the team leader and shall participate in the inspection by:

a. Attending pre-inspection conferences when and if scheduled.

b. Participating in the entire on-site inspection as permitted by agency priorities.

c. Providing support, as agreed upon with the team leader, in the preparation of specific sections of the inspection report where the field analyst or headquarters participant's expertise is especially useful.

Any difficulties involving field analysts or headquarters participants in the inspection should be discussed with District management and, if not resolved, immediately referred to the HFC-130 contact for this program.

CP 7348.808

E. Joint Inspections with Other Government Agency Personnel

Joint inspections with other government agency personnel may be conducted under this program. In all instances, the FDA field investigator will serve as the team leader. Specific instructions for conducting EPA data audits are provided in Compliance Program 7348.808A.

F. Confirmation of Schedule

All inspections of commercial laboratories are to be conducted without prior notification unless otherwise instructed by the assigning Center. Arrangements to conduct the initial inspection of university and government laboratories should be made soon after the laboratory has received the notification letter from the Bioresearch Monitoring Program Coordinator.

G. Field Responsibilities

Alert the Bioresearch Monitoring Program Coordinator to facilities that are becoming operational under GLPs. Notify the Center contact identified in the assignment when an inspection has been scheduled (preferably a week or more prior to the start of the inspection) or of any significant delay or postponement of an inspection assignment.

Part III – Inspectional

A. General Instructions

1. The investigator will **determine** the current state of GLP compliance by evaluating the laboratory facilities, operations, and study performance as outlined in Parts III, C, and D of this program.

2. Organization Chart - If the facility maintains an organization chart, **obtain** a current version of the chart for use during the inspection and **submit** it in the EIR.

3. Facility Floor-plan Diagram – **Obtain** a diagram of the facility. The diagram may identify areas that are not used for GLP activities. If it does not, request that appropriate facility personnel identify any areas that are not used for GLP activities. Use during the inspection and **submit** it in the EIR.

4. Master Schedule Sheet - **Obtain** a copy of the firm's master schedule sheet for all studies listed since the last GLP inspection or last two years and select studies as defined in 21 CFR 58.3(d). If the inspection is the first inspection of the facility, review the entire master schedule. If studies are identified as non-GLP, **determine** the nature of several studies to verify the accuracy of this designation. See 21 CFR 58.1 and 58.3(d). In contract laboratories **determine** who decides if a study is a GLP study.

5. Identification of Studies

   a. Directed Inspections – Inspection assignments will identify studies to be audited.

   b. Surveillance inspections – Inspection assignments may identify one or more studies to be audited. If the assignment does not identify a study for coverage, or if the referenced study is not suitable to assess all portions of current GLP compliance, the investigator will select studies as necessary to evaluate all areas of laboratory operations. When additional studies are selected, first priority should be given to FDA studies for submission to the assigning Center. **NOTE:** Studies performed for submission to other government agencies, e.g., Environmental Protection Agency, National Toxicology Program, National Cancer Institute, etc., will not be audited without authorization from the Bioresearch Monitoring Program Coordinator (HFC-230). However, this authorization is not necessary to briefly look at one of these studies to assess the ongoing operations of a portion of the facility.

      1. Criteria for selecting on-going and completed studies

         a. Safety studies conducted on FDA-regulated products that have been initiated or completed since the last GLP inspection.

         b. Safety studies that encompass the full scope of laboratory operations.

         c. Studies that are significant to safety assessment, e.g. carcinogenicity, reproductive toxicity, chronic toxicity studies.

         d. Studies in several species of animals.

C P 7348.808

The investigator is encouraged to contact the Center for guidance on study selection.

2. Ongoing Studies - **Obtain** a copy of the study protocol and **determine** the schedule of activities that will be underway during the inspection. This information should be used to schedule inspections of on-going laboratory operations, as well as equipment and facilities associated with the study. If there are no activities underway in a given area for the study selected, evaluate the area based on on-going activities.

3. Completed Studies - The data audit should be carried out as outlined in Part III, D. If possible, accompany laboratory personnel when they retrieve the study data to assess the adequacy of data retention, storage, and retrieval as described in Part III, C 10.

B. Areas of Expertise of the Facility

Testing facilities may conduct one or more types of studies within the scope of GLP regulations. The field investigator should **identify** in the EIR the types of studies conducted at the facility using the following broad categories:

1. Physical-chemical testing

2. Toxicity studies

3. Mutagenicity studies

4. Tissue residue depletion studies

5. Analytical and clinical chemistry testing

6. Other studies (specify)

C. Establishment Inspections

The facility inspection should be guided by the GLP regulations. The following areas should be evaluated and described as appropriate.

1. Organization and Personnel (21 CFR 58.29, 58.31, 58.33)

   a. Purpose: To determine whether the organizational structure is appropriate to ensure that studies are conducted in compliance with GLP regulations, and to determine whether management, study directors, and laboratory personnel are fulfilling their responsibilities under the GLPs.

b. Management Responsibilities (21 CFR 58.31) – Identify the various organizational units, their role in carrying out GLP study activities, and the management responsible for these organizational units. This includes identifying personnel who are performing duties at locations other than the test facility and identifying their line of authority. If the facility has an organization chart, much of this information can be determined from the chart.

Determine if management has procedures for assuring that the responsibilities in 58.31 can be carried out. Look for evidence of management involvement, or lack thereof, in the following areas:

1. Assigning and replacing study directors.

2. Control of study director workload (use the Master Schedule to assess workload).

3. Establishment and support of the Quality Assurance Unit (QAU), including assuring that deficiencies reported by the QAU are communicated to the study directors and acted upon.

4. Assuring that test and control articles or mixtures are appropriately tested for identity, strength, purity, stability, and uniformity.

5. Assuring that all study personnel are informed of and follow any special test and control article handling and storage procedures.

6. Providing required study personnel, resources, facilities, equipment, and materials.

7. Reviewing and approving protocols and standard operating procedures (SOPs).

8. Providing GLP or appropriate technical training.

c. Personnel (21 CFR 58.29) - Identify key laboratory and management personnel, including any consultants or contractors used, and review personnel records, policies, and operations to **determine** if:

C P 7348.808

1. Summaries of training and position descriptions are maintained and are current for selected employees.

2. Personnel have been adequately trained to carry out the study functions that they perform.

3. Personnel have been trained in GLPs.

4. Practices are in place to ensure that employees take necessary health precautions, wear appropriate clothing, and report illnesses to avoid contamination of the test and control articles and test systems.

   If the firm has computerized operations, **determine** the following (See also attachment A):

   a. Who was involved in the design, development, and validation of the computer system?

   b. Who is responsible for the operation of the computer system, including inputs, processing, and output of data?

   c. Whether computer system personnel have training commensurate with their responsibilities, including professional training and training in GLPs?

   d. Whether some computer system personnel are contractors who are present on-site full-time, or nearly full-time. The investigation should include these contractors as though they were employees of the firm. Specific inquiry may be needed to identify these contractors, as they may not appear on organization charts.

   e. Interview and observe personnel using the computerized systems to assess their training and performance of assigned duties.

d. Study director (21 CFR 58.33)

1. Assess the extent of the study director's actual involvement and participation in the study. In those instances when the study director is located off-site, review any correspondence/records between the testing facility management and quality assurance unit and the off-site study director. **Determine** that the study director is being kept immediately apprised of any problems that may affect the quality and integrity of the study.

2. Assess the procedures by which the study director:

   a. Assures the protocol and any amendments have been properly approved and are followed.

   b. Assures that all data are accurately recorded and verified.

   c. Assures that data are collected according to the protocol and SOPs.

   d. Documents unforeseen circumstances that may affect the quality and integrity of the study and implements corrective action.

   e. Assures that study personnel are familiar with and adhere to the study protocol and SOPs.

   f. Assures that study data are transferred to the archives at the close of the study.

   e. EIR Documentation and Reporting - Collect exhibits to document deficiencies. This may include SOPs, organizational charts, position descriptions, and CVs, as well as study-related memos, records, and reports for the studies selected for review. **The use of outside or contract facilities must be noted in the EIR. The assigning Center should be contacted for guidance on inspection of these facilities.**

2. Quality Assurance Unit (QAU; 21 CFR 58.35)

   a. Purpose: To determine if the test facility has an effective, independent QAU that monitors significant study events and facility operations, reviews records and reports, and assures management of GLP compliance.

   b. QAU Operations - (21 CFR 58.35(b-d)) - Review QAU SOPs to assure that they cover all methods and procedures for carrying out the required QAU functions, and confirm that they are being followed. **Verify** that SOPs exist and are being followed for QAU activities including, but not limited to, the following:

      1. Maintenance of a master schedule sheet.

      2. Maintenance of copies of all protocols and amendments.

      3. Scheduling of its in-process inspections and audits.

4. Inspection of each nonclinical laboratory study at intervals adequate to assure the integrity of the study, and maintenance of records of each inspection.

5. Immediately notify the study director and management of any problems that are likely to affect the integrity of the study.

6. Submission of periodic status reports on each study to the study director and management.

7. Review of the final study report.

8. Preparation of a statement to be included in the final report that specifies the dates inspections were made and findings reported to management and to the study director.

9. Inspection of computer operations.

Verify that, for any given study, the QAU is entirely separate from and independent of the personnel engaged in the conduct and direction of that study. Evaluate the time QAU personnel spend in performing in-process inspection and final report audits. **Determine** if the time spent is sufficient to detect problems in critical study phases and if there are adequate personnel to perform the required functions.

NOTE: The investigator may request the firm's management to certify in writing that inspections are being implemented, performed, documented, and followed-up in accordance with this section (See 58.35(d)).

c. EIR Documentation and Reporting - **Obtain** a copy of the master schedule sheet dating from the last routine GLP inspection or covering the past two years. If the master schedule is too voluminous, **obtain** representative pages to permit headquarters review. When master schedule entries are coded, **obtain** the code key. Deficiencies should be fully reported and documented in the EIR. Documentation to support deviations may include copies of QAU SOPs, list of QAU personnel, their curriculum vitae (CVs) or position descriptions, study-related records, protocols, and final reports.

3. Facilities (21 CFR 58.41 - 51)

a. Purpose: Assess whether the facilities are of adequate size and design.

b. Facility Inspection

1. Review environmental controls and monitoring procedures for critical areas (i.e., animal rooms, test article storage areas, laboratory areas, handling of bio-hazardous material, etc.) and **determine** if they appear adequate and are being followed.

2. Review the SOPs that identify materials used for cleaning critical areas and equipment, and assess the facility's current cleanliness.

3. **Determine** whether there are appropriate areas for the receipt, storage, mixing, and handling of the test and control articles.

4. **Determine** whether separation is maintained in rooms where two or more functions requiring separation are performed.

5. **Determine** that computerized operations and archived computer data are housed under appropriate environmental conditions (e.g., protected from heat, water, and electromagnetic forces).

c. EIR Documentation and Reporting - Identify which facilities, operations, SOPs, etc., were inspected. Only significant changes in the facility from previous inspections need be described. Facility floor plans may be collected to illustrate problems or changes. Document any conditions that would lead to contamination of test articles or to unusual stress of test systems.

4. Equipment (21 CFR 58.61 - 63)

a. Purpose: To assess whether equipment is appropriately designed and of adequate capacity and is maintained and operated in a manner that ensures valid results.

b. Equipment Inspection - Assess the following:

1. The general condition, cleanliness, and ease of maintenance of equipment in various parts of the facility.

2. The heating, ventilation, and air conditioning system design and maintenance, including documentation of filter changes and temperature/humidity monitoring in critical areas.

3. Whether equipment is located where it is used and that it is located in a controlled environment, when required.

4. Non-dedicated equipment for preparation of test and control article carrier mixtures is cleaned and decontaminated to prevent cross contamination.

5. For representative pieces of equipment check the availability of the following:

   a. SOPS and/or operating manuals.

   b. Maintenance schedule and log.

   c. Standardization/calibration procedure, schedule, and log.

   d. Standards used for calibration and standardization.

6. For computer systems, assess that the following procedures exist and are documented (See also attachment A):

   a. Validation study, including validation plan and documentation of the plan's completion.

   b. Maintenance of equipment, including storage capacity and back-up procedures.

   c. Control measures over changes made to the computer system, which include the evaluation of the change, necessary test design, test data, and final acceptance of the change.

   d. Evaluation of test data to assure that data are accurately transmitted and handled properly when analytical equipment is directly interfaced to the computer.

   e. Procedures for emergency back-up of the computer system (e.g., back-up battery system and data forms for recording data in the event of a computer failure or power outage).

c. EIR Documentation and Reporting - The EIR should list which equipment, records, and procedures were inspected and the studies to which they are related. Detail any deficiencies that might result in contamination of test articles, uncontrolled stress to test systems, and/or erroneous test results.

5. Testing Facility Operations (21 CFR 58.81)

    a. Purpose: To determine if the facility has established and follows written SOPs necessary to carry out study operations in a manner designed to ensure the quality and integrity of the data.

    b. SOP Evaluation

        1. Review the SOP index and representative samples of SOPs to ensure that written procedures exist to cover at least all of the areas identified in 58.81(b).

        2. **Verify** that only current SOPs are available at the personnel workstations.

        3. **Review** key SOPs in detail and check for proper authorization signatures and dates, and general adequacy with respect to the content (i.e., SOPs are clear, complete, and can be followed by a trained individual).

        4. **Verify** that changes to SOPs are properly authorized and dated and that a historical file of SOPs is maintained.

        5. **Ensure** that there are procedures for familiarizing employees with SOPs.

        6. **Determine** that there are SOPs to ensure the quality and integrity of data, including input (data checking and verification), output (data control), and an audit trail covering all data changes.

        7. **Verify** that a historical file of outdated or modified computer programs is maintained. If the firm does not maintain old programs in digital form, ensure that a hard copy of all programs has been made and stored.

        8. **Verify** that SOPs are periodically reviewed for current applicability and that they are representative of the actual procedures in use.

        9. Review selected SOPs and observe employees performing the operation to evaluate SOP adherence and familiarity.

    c. EIR Documentation and Reporting - Submit SOPs, data collection forms, and raw data records as exhibits that are necessary to support and illustrate deficiencies.

6. Reagents and Solutions (21 CFR 58.83)

C P 7348.808

    a. Purpose: To determine that the facility ensures the quality of reagents at the time of receipt and subsequent use.

        1. Review the procedures used to purchase, receive, label, and determine the acceptability of reagents and solutions for use in the studies.

        2. Verify that reagents and solutions are labeled to indicate identity, titer or concentration, storage requirements, and expiration date.

        3. Verify that for automated analytical equipment, the profile data accompanying each batch of control reagents are used.

        4. Check that storage requirements are being followed.

7. Animal Care (21 CFR 58.90)

    a. Purpose: To assess whether animal care and housing is adequate to minimize stress and uncontrolled influences that could alter the response of test system to the test article.

    b. Inspect the animal room(s) housing the study to observe operations, protocol and SOP adherence, and study records. **Refer to IOM 145.2 prior to inspecting sub-human primate facilities**.

        1. **Determine** that there are adequate SOPs covering environment, housing, feeding, handling, and care of laboratory animals, and that the SOPs and the protocol instructions are being followed.

        2. Review pest-control procedures and documentation of the chemicals used. Identify individuals responsible for the program. When a contractor provides the pest control, **determine** if someone from the laboratory accompanies the exterminator at all times.

        3. **Determine** whether the facility has an Institutional Animal Care and Use Committee (IACUC). Obtain and submit a copy of the Committee's Standard Operating Procedures and the most recent committee minutes to verify committee operation.

        4. **Determine** that all newly received animals are appropriately isolated, identified, and their health status is evaluated.

5. **Verify** that treatment given to animals that become diseased is authorized by the study director and documented.

6. For a representative sample of animals, compare individual animal identification against corresponding housing unit identification and dose group designations to assure that animals are appropriately identified.

7. For a representative sample of animals, review daily observation logs and **verify** their accuracy for animals reported as dead or having external gross lesions or masses.

8. Ensure that animals of different species, or animals of the same species on different projects, are separated as necessary.

9. **Verify** that cages, racks, and accessory equipment are cleaned and sanitized, and that appropriate bedding is used.

10. **Determine** that feed and water samples are collected at appropriate sources, analyzed periodically, and that analytical documentation is maintained.

c. EIR Documentation and Reporting - The EIR should identify which areas, operations, SOPs, studies, etc., were inspected and document any deficiencies.

8. Test and Control Articles (21 CFR 58.105 - 113)

a. Purpose: To determine that procedures exist to assure that test and control articles and mixtures of articles with carriers meet protocol specifications throughout the course of the study, and that accountability is maintained.

b. Characterization and Stability of Test Articles (21 CFR 58.105) - The responsibility for carrying out appropriate characterization and stability testing may be assumed by the facility performing the study or by the study sponsor. *When test article characterization and stability testing is performed by the sponsor, verify that the test facility has received documentation that this testing has been conducted.*

1. **Verify** that procedures are in place to ensure that:

C P 7348.808

a. The acquisition, receipt and storage of test articles, and means used to prevent deterioration and contamination are as specified.

b. The identity, strength, purity, and composition, (i.e., characterization) to define the test and control articles are determined for each batch and are documented.

c. The stability of test and control articles is documented.

d. The transfer of samples from the point of collection to the analytical laboratory is documented.

e. Storage containers are appropriately labeled and assigned for the duration of the study.

f. Reserve samples of test and control articles for each batch are retained for studies lasting more than four weeks.

c. Test and Control Article Handling (21 CFR 58.107)

1. **Determine** that there are adequate procedures for:

   a. Documentation for receipt and distribution.

   b. Proper identification and storage.

   c. Precluding contamination, deterioration, or damage during distribution.

2. Inspect test and control article storage areas to **verify** that environmental controls, container labeling, and storage are adequate.

3. Observe test and control article handling and identification during the distribution and administration to the test system.

4. Review a representative sample of accountability records and, if possible, **verify** their accuracy by comparing actual amounts in the inventory. For completed studies **verify** documentation of final test and control article reconciliation.

d. Mixtures of Articles with Carriers (58.113) - If possible, observe the preparation, sampling, testing, storage, and administration of mixtures. **Verify** that analytical tests are conducted, as appropriate, to:

1. Determine uniformity of mixtures and to determine periodically the concentration of the test or control article in the mixture, and

2. Determine the stability as required under study conditions.

Verify that the results are reported to the study director. When the sponsor performs analytical testing, concentration data may be reported to the study director as absolute or relative (percent of theoretical) values.

e. EIR Documentation and Reporting - Identify the test articles, SOPs, facilities, equipment, operations, etc., inspected. Review the analytical raw data versus the reported results for accuracy of reporting and overall integrity of the data that is being collected. Where deficiencies or other information suggest a problem with the purity, identity, strength, etc., of the test article or the concentration of test article mixtures, document and obtain copies of the analytical raw data and any related reports. Consideration should be given to collecting a sample as described in Part III, G.

9. Protocol and Conduct of Nonclinical Laboratory Study (21 CFR 58.120 - 130)

a. Purpose: To determine if study protocols are properly written and authorized, and that studies are conducted in accordance with the protocol and SOPs.

b. Study Protocol (21 CFR 58.120)

1. Review SOPs for protocol preparation and approval and **verify** they are followed.

2. Review the protocol to **determine** if it contains required elements.

3. Review all changes, revisions, or amendments to the protocol to ensure that they are authorized, signed, and dated by the study director.

4. **Verify** that all copies of the approved protocol contain all changes, revisions, or amendments.

c. Conduct of the Nonclinical Laboratory Study (21 CFR 58.130) - Evaluate the following laboratory operations, facilities, and equipment to **verify** conformity with protocol and SOP requirements for:

C P 7348.808

1. Test system monitoring.

2. Recording of raw data (manual and automated).

3. Corrections to raw data (corrections must not obscure the original entry and must be dated, initialed, and explained).

4. Randomization of test systems.

5. Collection and identification of specimens.

6. Authorized access to data and computerized systems.

d. EIR Reporting and Documentation - **Identify** the study(ies) inspected and, if available, the associated FDA research or marketing permit numbers. Report and document any deficiencies observed. **Submit**, as exhibits, a copy of all protocols and amendments that were reviewed.

10. Records and Reports (21 CFR 58.185 - 195)

a. Purpose: To assess how the test facility stores and retrieves raw data, documentation, protocols, final reports, and specimens.

b. Reporting of Study Results (21 CFR 58.185) - **Determine** if the facility prepares a final report for each study conducted. For selected studies, **obtain** the final report, and **verify** that it contains the following:

1. The required elements in 21 CFR 58.185(a)(1-14), including the identity (name and address) of any subcontractor facilities and portion of the study contracted, and a description of any computer program changes.

2. Dated signature of the study director (21 CFR 58.185(b)).

3. Corrections or additions to the final report are made in compliance with 21 CFR 58.185(c).

c. Storage and Retrieval of Records and Data (21 CFR 58.190)

1. **Verify** that raw data, documentation, protocols, final reports, and specimens have been retained.

2. **Identify** the individual responsible for the archives. Determine if delegation of duties to other individuals in maintaining the archives has occurred.

3.   **Verify** that archived material retained or referred to in the archives is indexed to permit expedient retrieval. It is not necessary that all data and specimens be in the same archive location. For raw data and specimens retained elsewhere, the archives index must make specific reference to those other locations.

4.   **Verify** that access to the archives is controlled and **determine** that environmental controls minimize deterioration.

5.   Ensure that there are controlled procedures for adding or removing material. Review archive records for the removal and return of data and specimens. Check for unexplained or prolonged removals.

6.   **Determine** how and where computer data and backup copies are stored, that records are indexed in a way to allow access to data stored on electronic media, and that environmental conditions minimize deterioration.

7.   **Determine** to what electronic media such as tape cassettes or ultra high capacity portable discs the test facility has the capacity of copying records in electronic form. **Report** names and identifying numbers of both copying equipment type and electronic medium type to enable agency personnel to bring electronic media to future inspections for collecting exhibits.

d.   EIR Documentation and Reporting – Provide a brief summary of the facility's report preparation procedures and their retention and retreival of records, reports, and specimens. If records are archived off-site, **obtain** a copy of documentation of the records which were transferred and where they are located. Describe and document deficiencies.

D. Data Audit

In addition to the procedures outlined above for evaluating the overall GLP compliance of a firm, the inspection should include the audit of at least one completed study. Studies for audit may be assigned by the Center or selected by the investigator as described in Part III, A. The audit will include a comparison of the protocol (including amendments to the protocol), raw data, records, and specimens against the final report to substantiate that protocol requirements were met and that findings were fully and accurately reported.

1. For each study audited, the study records should be reviewed for quality to ensure that data are:

    a. ***Attributable*** – the raw data can be traced, by signature or initials and date to the individual observing and recording the data. Should more than one individual observe or record the data, that fact should be reflected in the data.

    b. ***Legible*** – the raw data are readable and recorded in a permanent medium. If changes are made to original entries, the changes:

        1. Must not obscure the original entry.

        2. Indicate the reason for change.

        3. Must be signed or initialed and dated by the person making the change.

    c. ***Contemporaneous*** – the raw data are recorded at the time of the observation.

    d. ***Original*** – the first recording of the data.

    e. ***Accurate*** – the raw data are true and complete observations. For data entry forms that require the same data to be entered repeatedly, all fields should be completed or a written explanation for any empty fields should be retained with the study records.

2. General

    a. Determine if there were any significant changes in the facilities, operations, and QAU functions other than those previously reported.

    b. Determine whether the equipment used was inspected, standardized, and calibrated prior to, during, and after use in the study. If equipment malfunctioned, review the remedial action, and ensure that the final report addresses whether the malfunction affected the study.

    c. Determine if approved SOPs existed during the conduct of the study.

    d. Compare the content of the protocol with the requirements in 21 CFR 58.120.

e. Review the final report for the study director's dated signature and the QAU statement as required in 21 CFR 58.35(b)(7).

3. Protocol vs. Final Report - Study methods described in the final report should be compared against the protocol and the SOPs to confirm those requirements were met. Examples include, but are not limited to, the following:

a. Selection and acquisition of the test system, i.e., species, source, weight range, number, age, date ordered, date received.

b. Procedure for receipt, examination, and isolation of newly received animals.

c. Methods of test system identification, housing, and assignment to study.

d. Types and occurrences of diseases and clinical observations prior to and during the study, as well as any treatments administered.

e. Frequency and methods of sampling and analysis for contaminants in feed and water.

f. Feed and water contaminant levels did not exceed limits specified in the protocol.

g. Types of bedding and pest control materials do not interfere with the study.

h. Preparation and administration of test and/or control articles.

i. Analysis of test article/test article carrier mixtures.

j. Observation of the test system response to test article.

k. Handling of dead or moribund animals.

l. Collection and analysis of specimens and raw data.

m. Necropsy, gross pathology, and histopathology.

4. Final Report vs. Raw Data

a. The audit should include a detailed review of records, memorandum, and other raw data to confirm that the findings in the final report completely and accurately reflect the raw data. Representative samples of raw data should be

C P 7348.808

audited against the final report. Examples of types of data to be checked include, but are not limited to, the following:

1. Animal body weight records.

2. Food and water consumption records.

3. Test system observation and dosing records.

4. Records for the analysis of uniformity, concentration, and stability of test and control article mixtures.

5. Protocol-required analyses (e.g., urinalysis, hematology, blood chemistry, ophthalmologic exams).

6. Necropsy and gross pathology records.

7. Histopathology, including records for tissue processing and slide preparation.

8. Conformity between "interim" reports (e.g., a report on the first year of a multi-year study) and the final report.

b. A representative number of animals from selected dose groups (initially the control and high) should be traced from receipt through final histopathologic examination. Evaluate for the following:

1. The accuracy of individual test system identification.

2. Review trends in each parameter measured or observed and note inconsistencies.

3. Explanations for reported data outliers.

4. Conformity between *in vivo* test system observations and gross pathology observations.

5. Conformity between gross pathology observations and histopathologic examinations.

6. Documentation of unforeseen circumstances that may have affected the quality and integrity of the study.

5. Specimens vs. Final Report - The audit should include examination of a representative sample of specimens in the archives for confirmation of the number and identity of specimens in the final report.

6. EIR Documentation and Reporting

    a. All studies audited should be identified by:

        1. Sponsor's name.

        2. Study title (and any study numbers).

        3. Study director's name.

        4. Test article name and/or code.

        5. Test system.

        6. The date the protocol was signed by the study director.

        7. In-life starting and ending dates.

        8. The date the study director signed the final report. and if available,

        9. The FDA research or marketing application number.

    b. Describe and document any significant deficiencies in the conduct or reporting of the study. **Obtain** a copy of the narrative study report and protocol.

E. Refusal to Permit Inspection

Field investigators should refer to IOM Section 514 for general guidance on dealing with refusal to permit inspection. Test facility management should be advised that the agency will not consider a nonclinical laboratory study in support of a research or marketing permit if the testing facility refuses to permit inspection (58.15(b)).

Refusal to permit inspection of facilities or studies should be reported immediately by telephone to the bioresearch monitoring program coordinator (hfc-230), (301- 827-0425), and followed-up by fax to hfc-230 (301-827-0482) with an information copy to the assigning center.

Under this program, partial refusals, including refusal to permit access to, and copying of the master schedule (including any code sheets), SOPs, and other documents pertaining to the inspection will be treated as a **"total"** refusal to permit inspection.

F. Sealing of Research Records

Whenever a field investigator encounters questionable or suspicious records under any Bioresearch Monitoring Program, and is unable to copy or review them immediately, and has reason for preserving the integrity of those records, **the investigator is to immediately contact by telephone HFC-230 for instructions**. Refer to IOM 453.7 for more information.

G. Samples

1. Collection of samples should be considered when the situation under audit or surveillance suggests that the facility had, or is having, problems in the area of characterization, stability, storage, contamination, or dosage preparation. **The investigator should contact the assigning Center and the Division of Field Science (HFC-140) before samples are collected.** If the field investigator collects a sample, a copy of the methodology and reference samples from the sponsor or the testing facility must also be **obtained**. The copy will be sent to HFC-140 for designation of a laboratory to perform the sample analysis according to instrument capabilities and the availability of the selected district laboratory. The investigator should contact HFC-140 at (301) 827-7605 for specific disposition/handling instructions. The investigator must use the appropriate 7-digit code for product collected and provide complete documentation with each sample for possible legal/administrative actions.

2. Samples may include physical samples of:

   a. Carrier.

   b. Test article.

   c. Control article.

   d. Mixtures of test or control articles with carriers.

   e. Specimens including wet tissues, tissue blocks, and slides (see above regarding Center and HFC-140 authorization and instructions).

H. Inspectional Observations

A FDA 483 listing inspectional observations will be issued under this program. Findings should not be listed on the FDA 483 if in the opinion of the field investigator:

1. The findings are problems that have been observed and corrected by the firm through its internal procedures.

2. The findings are minor and are one-time occurrences that have no impact on the firm's operations, study conduct, or data integrity.

Findings that are not considered significant enough to be listed on the FDA 483 may be discussed with the firm's management. Such discussions must be reported in the EIR.

I. Establishment Inspection Reports

Because the Centers are solely responsible for issuing post-inspection correspondence, each EIR must include the full name, title, academic degree(s), and mailing address of the most responsible person at the test facility (For universities the most responsible person would typically be a member of the administration (e.g., department chair, dean)).

Documentation necessary to support the observations listed on the FDA 483 should be collected, **submitted**, and referenced in the EIR narrative. Suspected violations under Title 21 must be documented sufficiently to form the basis for legal or administrative action. Discuss potential violations under Title 18 with your supervisor and District compliance officer prior to extensive documentation.

C P 7348.808

1. Full Reporting

A full report will be **prepared** and **submitted** in the following situations:

a. The initial GLP inspection of a facility.

b. All inspections that may result in an OAI classification.

c. Any assignment specifically requesting a full report.

The EIR should contain the headings described in IOM 593.3, in addition to the headings outlined in Part III, C, and D. The report must always include sufficient information and documentation to support the recommended classification.

2. Abbreviated Reporting

a. Field investigators may use abbreviated reporting for the following types of assignments:

1. Surveillance inspections (except for initial inspections) of a facility when it is apparent from the findings that the inspection may result in a final classification of NAI or

VAI. These reports must include enough documented information to support the final classification.

2. Directed inspections and data audits provided the report fully covers all aspects of the specific topic of the inspection (i.e., operations, past deficiencies, assigned studies, etc.) and documents significant adverse findings to support the final classification.

b. Format

1. **The EIR should be clearly identified as an abbreviated report.**

2. The report should include all the headings described in IOM section 593.1 and include:

   a. The identity of the studies selected for audit and review

   b. Identification of the areas, operations, and amount of data that were inspected (e.g., identity and percent of records reviewed in a specific area, number of animals tracked, percent of slides checked for accountability, etc.)

   c. All adverse observations will be fully discussed in the EIR and documented to permit assessment of their impact on the quality and integrity of the studies.

If the Center review reveals that an abbreviated report is inadequate, the Center will notify HFC-130 that additional information is required.

Part IV - Analytical

A. Analyzing Laboratories

All field and headquarters laboratories.

B. Analysis

Samples of test or control articles, or mixtures thereof, may be submitted for a determination for identity, strength, potency, purity, or composition. Sample analysis will follow the exact methodology of the sponsor or the testing facility. If the methodology is available at the testing facility, the field investigator must submit the methodology with the sample. In those cases where a contract testing facility does not have the methodology, the field investigator should direct the facility to request the method be provided to the district laboratory by the sponsor.

C. Identification of Appropriate District Laboratory

Contact ORO, Division of Field Science (HFC-140) at (301) 827-7065.

D. Reporting

The analyzing laboratory will submit copies of the Collection Report and the Analytical Worksheets to the originating District Office and to the Center with reference to the EIR.

Part V - Regulatory / Administrative Strategy

A. District EIR Classification Authority

The District is encouraged to review and initially classify EIRs under this compliance program.

B. Center EIR Classification Authority

The Center has the **final** classification authority for all Bioresearch Monitoring Program inspection reports. The Center will provide to the District copies of all final classifications, including any reason for changes from the initial classification.

C. EIR Classifications

The following guidance is to be used in conjunction with the instructions in FMD-86 for initial District and Center classification of EIRs generated under this compliance program:

1. NAI - No objectionable conditions or practices were found during the inspection (or the objectionable conditions found do not justify further regulatory action).

2. VAI - Objectionable conditions or practices were found, but the agency is not prepared to take or recommend any administrative or regulatory action.

3. OAI - Regulatory and/or administrative actions will be recommended.

C P 7348.808

D. Post-Inspectional Correspondence

Under the BIMO program the Centers are responsible for
administrative or regulatory follow-up. The District Office should
advise the Center of any response to the FDA 483 or any other
communication (written or oral) with the facility concerning the
inspection. Similarly, if the Center has communication with the facility
following the inspection the District should be advised of such
communication.

E. District Follow-up

All District follow-up action, including reinspection, will be made at
the request of the Center. On occasion, District compliance units may
initiate case development activities and may issue investigative
assignments whenever review of the inspection report raises the
possibility of severe violations of the FFD&C Act or other Federal
statutes. This intention is to be immediately communicated to the
Bioresearch Monitoring Program Coordinator (HFC-230).

F. Regulatory/Administrative Actions

The regulatory/administrative actions that can be used under this
compliance program are not mutually exclusive. Follow-up of an OAI
inspection may involve the use of one or more of the following:

1. Warning Letter

2. Re-inspection

3. Informal conference

4. Third party validation of a nonclinical study or studies

5. Rejection of a nonclinical study or studies

6. Disqualification of the facility

7. Injunction/prosecution

8. Withholding or revocation of marketing permit

9. Termination of a research permit

10. Application integrity policy

Part VI - References And Contacts

A. References

1. Guide for the Care and Use of Laboratory Animals, DHHS Publication No. (NIH) 96-23

2. The Animal Welfare Act, 9 CFR Parts 1, 2, 3

3. 21 CFR 11 - Electronic Records. Electronic Signatures Regulation effective August 1997.

4. 21 CFR 58.1 - 58.219 Good Laboratory Practice Regulations effective June 1979, and amended effective October 1987

5. Good Laboratory Practice Regulations, Management Briefings, Post Conference Report, August 1979

6. Good Laboratory Practice Regulations, Questions and Answers, June 1981

7. "Toxicological Principles for the Safety Assessment of Direct Food Additives and Color Additives used in Food," FDA, Bureau of Foods

8. "Guide to Inspection of Computerized Systems in Drug Processing," February 1983

9. "Software Development Activities, Technical Report" July 1987

10. "Guide For Detecting Fraud in Bioresearch Monitoring Inspections," April 1993

Copies of the listed references may be obtained from HFC-130.

B. Program Contacts

Questions regarding the interpretation of the regulations or agency policy should be addressed to the Bioresearch Monitoring Program Coordinator (HFC-230). When technical questions arise on a specific assignment, or when additional information or guidance is required, contact the assigning Center.

1. Specific Contacts

Office of the Associate Commissioner for Regulatory Affairs

Office of Enforcement, Division of Compliance Policy: Dr. James F. McCormack, HFC-230, 301-827-0425, FAX 301-827-0482.

Office of Regional Operations, Division of Emergency and Investigational Operations: Dr. Thaddeus Sze, HFC-130, 301-827-5649, FAX 301-827-6685.

Center for Drug Evaluation and Research (CDER)

Division of Scientific Investigations: Mr. Ty Fujiwara, HFD-48, 301-827-7287, FAX 301-594-1204.

Center for Biologics Evaluation and Research (CBER)

Bioresearch Monitoring Staff: Dr. Patricia Hasemann, HFM-664, 301-594-1077, FAX 301-827-6221.

Center for Veterinary Medicine (CVM)

Bioresearch Monitoring Staff: Ms. Dorothy Pocurull, HFV-234, 301-827-6664, FAX 301-827-1498.

Center for Devices and Radiological Health (CDRH)

Division of Bioresearch Monitoring: Mr. Rodney Allnutt, HFZ-311, 301-594-4723, FAX 301-594-4731.

Center for Food Safety and Applied Nutrition (CFSAN)

Division of Product Policy: Dr. John Welsh, HFS-207, 202-418-3057, FAX 202-418-3126.

Part VII – Headquarter's Responsibilities

A. Office of Regulatory Affairs

1. Division of Compliance Policy (HFC-230)

    a. Coordinates compliance policy and guidance development.

    b. Coordinates responses to inquiries regarding agency interpretation of regulations and policy.

    c. Serves as the liaison with other Federal agencies and foreign governments with whom FDA has Memoranda of Agreement or Memoranda of Understanding.

d.   Resolves issues involving compliance or enforcement policy.

e.   Advises and concurs with Centers on recommended administrative and regulatory actions.

f.   Coordinates the distribution and review of multi-center and inter-agency EIRs including the planning, coordination, and designation of a lead Center for EIR classification, issuance of correspondence, and follow-up assignments.

g.   Coordinates Center and other Federal agency inspection assignments.

h.   Coordinates modifications and future issuances of this compliance program.

i.   Prepares notice of first inspection letters to university and government laboratories.

2.   Division of Emergency and Investigational Operations (DEIO; HFC-130)

a.   Provides inspection quality assurance, training of field personnel, and operational guidance.

b.   Maintains liaison with Centers and Field Offices and resolves operational questions.

c.   Coordinates and schedules joint Center and multi-District inspections.

3.   Division of Field Science (DFS; HFC-140)

a.   Assigns laboratories for sample analysis and responds to method inquiries.

B. Centers

1.   Review EIRS and regulatory/administrative recommendations forwarded by the districts.

2.   Provide OE with a list of facilities on a quarterly basis, or as other priorities dictate, to be scheduled for inspection.

3.   Select studies to be audited and provide necessary support documents.

C P 7348.808

4. Prepare letters for issuance by the Center, ORA, or Commissioner as appropriate.

5. Issue all assignments to the field.

6. Recommend compliance program changes to OE.

7. Distribute copies of EIR correspondence to districts and OE.

8. Provide inspectional support to the field by direct participation and in consultant capacity.

9. Copy all Centers whenever a Warning Letter has issued to a specific laboratory.

Attachment A

Computerized Systems

The intent of this attachment is to collect, in one place, references to computer systems found throughout Part III. Computer systems and operations should be thoroughly covered during inspection of any facility. No additional reporting is required under this Attachment.

In August 1997, the Agency's regulation on electronic signatures and electronic recordkeeping became effective. The Regulation, at 21 CFR Part 11, describes the technical and procedural requirements that must be met if a firm chooses to maintain records electronically and/or use electronic signatures. Part 11 works in conjunction with other FDA regulations and laws that require recordkeeping. Those regulations and laws ("predicate rules") establish requirements for record content, signing, and retention.

Certain older electronic systems may not have been in full compliance with Part 11 by August 1997 and modification to these so called "legacy systems" may take more time. Part 11 does not grandfather legacy systems and FDA expects that firms using legacy systems are taking steps to achieve full compliance with Part 11.

If a firm is keeping electronic records or using electronic signatures, **determine** if they are in compliance with 21 CFR Part 11. **Determine** the depth of part 11 coverage on a case by case basis, in light of initial findings and program resources. At a minimum ensure that: (1) the firm has prepared a corrective action plan for achieving full compliance with part 11 requirements, and is making progress toward completing that plan in a timely manner; (2) accurate and complete electronic and human readable copies of electronic records, suitable for review, are made available; and (3) employees are held accountable and responsible for actions taken under their electronic signatures. If initial findings indicate the firm's electronic records and/or electronic signatures may not be trustworthy and reliable, or when electronic recordkeeping systems inhibit meaningful FDA inspection, a more detailed evaluation may be warranted. Districts should consult with center compliance officers and the Office of Enforcement (HFC-240) in assessing the need for, and potential depth of, more detailed part 11 coverage. When substantial and significant part 11 deviations exist, FDA will not accept use of electronic records and electronic signatures to meet the requirements of the applicable predicate rule. See Compliance Policy Guide (CGP), Sec. 160.850.

See IOM sections 594.1 and 527.3 for procedures for collecting and identifying electronic data.

Personnel - Part III, C.1.c. (21 CFR 58.29)

Determine the following:

- Who was involved in the design, development, and validation of the computer system?

- Who is responsible for the operation of the computer system, including inputs, processing, and output of data?

- If computer system personnel have training commensurate with their responsibilities, including professional training and training in GLPs.

- Whether some computer system personnel are contractors who are present on-site full-time, or nearly full-time. The investigation should include these contractors as though they were employees of the firm. Specific inquiry may be needed to identify these contractors, as they may not appear on organization charts.

QAU Operations - Part III, C.2 (21 CFR 58.35(b-d))

- **Verify** SOPs exist and are being followed for QAU inspections of computer operations.

Facilities - Part III, C.3 (21 CFR 58.41 - 51)

- **Determine** that computerized operations and archived computer data are housed under appropriate environmental conditions.

Equipment - Part III, C.4 (21 CFR 58.61 - 63)

For computer systems, check that the following procedures exist and are documented:

- Validation study, including validation plan and documentation of the plan's completion.

- Maintenance of equipment, including storage capacity and back-up procedures.

- Control measures over changes made to the computer system, which include the evaluation of the change, necessary test design, test data, and final acceptance of the change.

- Evaluation of test data to assure that data is accurately transmitted and handled properly when analytical equipment is directly interfaced to the computer. and

- Procedures for emergency back-up of the computer system, (e.g., back-up battery system and data forms for recording data in case of a computer failure or power outage).

Testing Facility Operations - Part III, C.5 (21 CFR 58.81)

- **Verify** that a historical file of outdated or modified computer programs is maintained.

Records and Reports (21 CFR 58.185 - 195) (PART III C.10.b.)

- **Verify** that the final report contains the required elements in 58.185(a)(1-14), including a description of any computer program changes.

Storage and Retrieval of Records and Data - Part III, C.10.c. (21 CFR 58.190)

- Assess archive facilities for degree of controlled access and adequacy of environmental controls with respect to computer media storage conditions.

- **Determine** how and where computer data and backup copies are stored, that records are indexed in a way to allow access to data stored on electronic media, and that environmental conditions minimize deterioration.

- **Determine** how and where original computer data and backup copies are stored.

Good Laboratory Practices Questions and Answers

Guidance for Industry

U.S. Department of Health and Human Services
Food and Drug administration Office of Regulatory affairs

June 1981 (Minor editorial and formatting changes made December 1999 & July 2007)

Since June 20, 1979, the agency has been asked many questions on the Good Laboratory Practice regulations (GLPs, 21 CFR 58). In accord with agency procedures, responses have been prepared and copies of the associated correspondence have been filed in the Dockets Management Branch (HFA-305). The responses have also been provided to the bioresearch monitoring program managers and to the district offices in order to ensure consistency of interpretation and equity of program operation. Unfortunately, the numerous filed correspondences contain many repeat questions that are not categorized to relate to the specific GLP subpart and section. On occasion, the answers appear to be somewhat cryptic. These disadvantages serve to limit the utility of the correspondences as advisories to our headquarters and field offices.

This document, therefore, consolidates all GLP questions answered by the agency during the past 2 years clarifies the questions and answers as needed, and relates the questions and answers to the specific pertinent provisions of the GLPs. It represents a digest of some 30 letters, 160 memoranda of telephone conversations, 34 memoranda of meetings and 30 miscellaneous correspondences that have been issued by agency personnel. The document does not duplicate questions and answers that were dealt with in the August, 1979 Post Conference Report on the Good Laboratory Practice Regulations Management Briefings.

This document should be reviewed by field investigators prior to making GLP inspections and by headquarters personnel involved in the GLP program. Questions should be directed to:

Bioresearch Monitoring Program Coordinator (HFC-130)
Food and Drug Administration
5600 Fishers Lane Rockville, MD 20857

Subpart A – General Provisions

Section 58.1 - Scope.

1. Do the GLPs apply to validation trials conducted to confirm the analytical methods used to determine the concentration of test article in animal tissues and drug dosage forms?

   No.

2. Do the GLPs apply to the following studies on animal health products: overdosage studies in the target species, animal safety studies in the target species, tissue residue accumulation and depletion studies, and udder irritation studies?

   Yes.

3. Do the GLPs apply to safety studies on cosmetic products?

   No. Such studies are not carried out in support of a marketing permit. However, the GLPs represent good quality control a goal that all testing facilities should strive to attain.

4. Do safety studies done to determine the potential drug-abuse characteristics of a test article have to be done under the GLPs?

   Yes they do, but only when the studies are required to be submitted to the agency as part of an application for a research or marketing permit.

5. Do the GLPs apply to the organoleptic evaluation of processed foods?

   No.

6. Do the GLPs apply to all of the analytical support work conducted to provide supplementary data to a safety study?

The GLPs apply to the chemical procedures used to characterize the test article, to determine the stability of the test article and its mixtures, and to determine the homogeneity and concentration of test article mixtures. Likewise, the GLPs apply to the chemical procedures used to analyze specimens (e.g. clinical chemistry, urinalysis). The GLPs do not apply to the work done to develop chemical methods of analysis or to establish the specifications of a test article.

7. Is it possible to obtain an exemption from specific provisions of the GLPs for special nonclinical laboratory studies?

    Yes. The GLPs were written with the aim of being applicable to a broad variety of studies, test articles and test systems. Nonetheless, the agency realizes that not all of the GLP provisions apply to all studies and, indeed, for some special studies certain of the GLP provisions may compromise proper science. For this reason, laboratories may petition the agency for exemption for certain studies from some of the GLP provisions. The petition should contain sufficient facts to justify granting the exemption.

8. Are subcontractor laboratories that furnish a particular service such as ophthalmology exams, reading of animal ECGs, EEGs, EMGs, preparation of blocks and slides from tissues, statistical analysis and hematology covered by the GLPs?

    Yes, to the extent that they contribute to a study that is subject to the GLPs.

Section 58.3 - Definitions.

1. Are animal cage cards considered to be raw data?

    Raw data is defined as "any laboratory worksheets, records, memorandum, notes that are the result of original observations and activities and are necessary for the reconstruction and evaluation of-the report of that study." Cage cards are not raw data if they contain information like animal number, study number, study dates, and cage number (information that is not the result of original observations and that is not necessary for study reconstruction). However, if an original observation is put on the cage cards, then all cards must be saved as raw data.

2. Are photocopies of raw data, which are dated and verified by signature of the copier, considered to be "exact" copies of the raw data?

   Yes.

3. Are records of quarantine, animal receipt, environmental monitoring, and instrument calibration considered to be raw data?

   Yes.

4. A laboratory conducts animal studies to establish a baseline set of data for a different test species/strain. No test article is administered but the toxicology laboratory facilities and procedures will be used and the resulting data may eventually be submitted do the agency as part of a research or marketing permit. Are the studies considered to be nonclinical laboratory studies that are covered by the GLPs?

   Generally, a nonclinical laboratory study involves a test article studied under laboratory conditions for the purpose of determining its safety. The cited example does not fit the definition so it would not be covered by the GLPs. Since the data from the baseline studies may be used to interpret the results of a nonclinical laboratory study, it is recommended, but not required, that the study be conducted in accord with GLPs in order to ensure valid baseline data.

5. The definition of "nonclinical laboratory study" excludes field trials in animals. What is a field trial in animals?

   A field trial in animals is similar to a human clinical trial. It is conducted for the purpose of obtaining data on animal drug efficacy and it is excluded from coverage under the GLPs.

6. Necropsies are done by prosectors trained by and working under the supervision of a pathologist. The necropsy data are recorded by the prosector on data sheets, and when making the final report, the pathologist summarizes the data collected by the prosector as well as by him/herself. What constitutes the raw data in this example?

Both the prosector's data sheets as well as the signed and dated report of the pathologist would be considered raw data.

7. Is a computer printout derived from data transferred to computer media from laboratory data sheets considered to be raw data?

    No.

8. Are the assay plates used in the 10t1/2 mammalian cell transformation assay considered to be specimens?

    Yes.

9. If a firm uses parapathologists to screen tissue preparations, are the parapathologists' data sheets considered to be raw data?

    Yes.

Section 58.10 Applicability to studies performed under grants and contracts.

1. Certain contracts specify that a series of nonclinical laboratory studies be done on a single test article. Do the GLPs permit the designation of different study directors for each study under the contract?

    Yes.

2. Do the GLPs require that a sponsor approve the study director for a contracted study?

    No. Testing facility management designates the study director.

3. A firm functions as a primary contractor for nonclinical laboratory studies. The actual studies are then subcontracted to nonclinical laboratories. Is the firm considered to be a "sponsor?"

    The GLPs define "sponsor" as a person who initiates and supports a nonclinical laboratory study. Sponsorship in the cited example would be determined by the specific provisions of the contract.

Q&A

4. Who is responsible for test article characterization - the sponsor or the contractor?

   The GLPs do not assign the responsibility in this area. The matter is a subject of the specific contractual arrangement between the sponsor and the contractor.

5. Do contract laboratories have to show the sponsor's name on the Master Schedule Sheet or can this information be coded?

   The information can be coded but the code must be revealed to the FDA investigator on request.

6. A sponsor desires to contract for a nonclinical laboratory study to be conducted in a foreign laboratory. Must the sponsor notify the foreign laboratory that compliance with the U.S. GLPs is required?

   Yes.

7. Must a contractor include in the final report information on test article characterization and stability when such information has been collected by the sponsor?

   No. The contractor should identify in its final report which information will be subsequently supplied by the sponsor.

8. Must a sponsor reveal toxicology data already collected on a test article to a contract laboratory?

   No. If use of the test article involves a potential danger to laboratory personnel, the contract laboratory should be advised so that appropriate precautions can be taken.

Section 58.15 Inspection of a testing facility.

1. What is the usual procedure for the issuance of a form FDA-483?

   The FDA-483 is the written notice of objectionable practices or deviations from the regulations that is prepared by the FDA investigator at the end of the inspection. The items listed on the form serve as the basis for the exit discussion with laboratory management at which time management can either agree or disagree with the items and can offer possible corrective actions to be taken. Management may also respond to the district office in writing after it has had sufficient time to properly study the FDA-483.

2. Will a laboratory subsequently be notified of GLP deviations not listed on the FDA-483?

    This does happen. The FDA investigator prepares an establishment inspection report (EIR) which summarizes the observations made at the laboratory and which contains exhibits concerning the studies audited (Protocols, SOPs, CV's, etc.). The EIR is then reviewed by District personnel as well as headquarters personnel. This review may reveal additional GLP deviations that should be and are communicated to laboratory management.

3. What kinds of domestic toxicology laboratory inspections does FDA perform and how frequently are they done?

    FDA performs four kinds of inspections related to the GLPs and nonclinical laboratory studies. These include: A GLP inspection an inspection undertaken as a periodic, routine determination of a laboratory's compliance with the GLPs, it includes examination of an ongoing study as well as a completed study; A data audit - an inspection made to verify that the information contained in a final report submitted to FDA is accurate and reflected by the raw data; A directed inspection any of a series of inspections conducted for various compelling reasons (questionable data in a final report, tips from informers, etc.); A follow-up inspection - an inspection made sometime after a GLP inspection which revealed objectionable practices and conditions. The purpose of the follow-up inspection is to assure that proper corrective actions have been taken. GLP inspections are scheduled once every two years whereas the other kinds of inspections are scheduled as needed.

4. Should GLP investigators comment on the scientific merits of a protocol or the scientific interpretation given in the final report?

    No. Their function is strictly a noting of observations and verification. Scientific judgments are made by the respective headquarters review units that deal with the test article.

5. Can a GLP EIR be reviewed by laboratory management prior to issuance?

> No. The GLP EIR is an internal agency document, which reflects the observations and findings of the FDA investigator. It can not be released to anyone outside the agency until agency action has been completed and the released copy is purged of all trade secret information. Laboratories that disagree with portions of the EIR should write a letter, which contains the areas of disagreement to the local FDA District Office. The laboratories can ask that their letters accompany the EIR whenever it is requested under the Freedom of Information Act.

6. Can FDA investigators take photographs of objectionable practices and conditions?

> It is the agency position that photographs can be taken as a part of the inspection and this position has been sustained by a District Court decision.

7. The GLP Compliance Program requires the FDA investigator to select an ongoing study in order to inspect current laboratory operations what criteria are used to select the study?

> The studies are selected in accord with agency priorities, i.e. the longest-term study on the most significant product.

8. Does FDA inspect international nonclinical laboratories once every two years?

> No. Overseas laboratories are scheduled for inspection on the basis of having submitted to FDA the results of significant studies on important products.

9. What background materials are used by agency investigators to prepare for a GLP inspection?

> Prior to an inspection, the following materials are usually reviewed:
>
> a. The GLP regulations;
>
> b. the Management Briefings Post-Conference Report;
>
> c. assorted memoranda and policy issuances;
>
> d. the GLP Compliance Program;

e.   the protocol of an ongoing study, if available;

f.   the final report of a completed study, if available;

g.   the inspection report of the most recent inspection.

10. How long does FDA allow a laboratory to effect corrective actions after an inspection has been made?

> If the results of an inspection reveal that significant deviations from the GLPs exist, the laboratory will be sent a regulatory letter that lists the major deviations and that requests a response within 10 days. The response should describe those actions that the laboratory has taken or plans to take to effect correction. The response should also encompass items that were listed on the FDA-483 and those that were discussed during the exit discussion with laboratory management. A specific timetable should be given for accomplishing the planned actions. The reasonableness of the timetable will be determined by FDA compliance staff, based on the needs of the particular situation.

> For less significant deviations, the laboratory will be sent a Notice of Adverse Findings letter that also lists the deviations but that requests a response within 30 days. Again, the reasonableness of the response will be determined by FDA staff.

11. Does a laboratory's responsibility for corrective action listed on a FDA-483 begin at the conclusion of an inspection or upon receipt of correspondence from the originating bureau in which corrective action is requested?

> The FDA-483 lists observations of violative conditions that have the capability to adversely affect nonclinical laboratory studies. Corrective actions should be instituted as soon as possible.

12. Does FDA preannounce all GLP inspections?

> Laboratory management is informed of all routine GLP inspections prior to the inspection, but special compliance or investigative inspections need not be pre-announced.

Q&A

Subpart B – Organization and Personnel

Section 58.29 - Personnel.

1. For what sequence in the supervisory chain should position descriptions be available?

   Position descriptions should be available for each individual engaged in or supervising the conduct of the study.

2. Should current summaries of training and experience list attendance at scientific and technical meetings?

   Yes. The agency considers such attendance as a valuable adjunct to the other kinds of training received by laboratory personnel.

3. If certain specialists (pathologists, statisticians, ophthalmologists, etc.) are contracted to conduct certain aspects of a study, need they be identified in the final report?

   Yes.

4. Does the QAU have to be composed of technical personnel?

   No. Management is however, responsible for assuring that "personnel clearly understand the functions they are to perform" (Section 58.31(f)) and that each individual engaged in the study has the appropriate combination of education, training and experience (Section 58.29(a)).

Section 58.31 - Testing Facility Management.

1. Can the study director be the chief executive of a nonclinical laboratory?

   No. The GLPs require that there be a separation of function between the study director and the QAU director. In the example, the QAU director would be reporting to the study director.

Section 58.33 Study director.

1. The GLPs permit the designation of an "acting" or "deputy" study director to be responsible for a study when the study

director is on leave. Should study records identify the designated "deputy" or "acting" study director?

Yes.

2. Is the study director responsible for adherence to the GLPs?

Yes.

Section 58.35 Quality Assurance Unit.

1. As a QAU person, I have no expertise in the field of pathology. How do I audit pathology findings?

> The QAU is not expected to perform a scientific evaluation of a study or to "second-guess" the scientific procedures that are used. QAU inspections are made to ensure that the GLPs, SOPs and protocols are being followed and that the data summarized in the final report accurately reflect the results of the study. A variety of procedures can be used to do this but certainly the procedures should include an examination and correlation of the raw data records.

2. Must the QAU keep copies of all protocols and amendments and SOPs and amendments?

> The QAU must keep copies of all protocols as currently amended. The only SOPs that the QAU are required to keep are those concerned with the operations and procedures of the QAU.

3. Does the QAU have to monitor compliance with regulations promulgated by other government agencies?

> The GLPs do not require this.

4. Can an individual who is involved in a nonclinical laboratory study perform QAU functions for portions of the study that the individual is not involved with?

> No. However, the individual can perform QAU functions for a study that he/she is not involved with.

5. Does the QAU review amendments to the final report?

> Yes.

Q&A

6. What studies are required to be listed on the master schedule sheet?

    The master schedule sheet should list all nonclinical laboratory studies conducted on FDA regulated products and intended to support an application for a research or marketing permit.

7. May the QAU in its periodic reports to management and the study director recommend actions to solve existing problems?

    Yes.

8. If raw data are transcribed and sent to the sponsor for (a) preparing the data in computer format or (b) performing a statistical analysis, what are the responsibilities of the QAU?

    For (a) the QAU should assure that the computer-formatted data accurately reflect the raw data. For (b) the statistical analyses would comprise a report from a participating scientist, therefore it should be checked by QAU and appended to the final report.

9. Can the QAU also be responsible for maintaining the laboratory archives?

    Yes.

10. Can a QAU be constituted as a single person?

    Yes, provided that the workload is not excessive and other duties do not prevent the person from doing an adequate job. It would be prudent to designate an alternate in case of disability, vacations, etc.

11. Who is responsible for defining study phases and designating critical study phases and can these be covered in the SOP?

    The GLPs do not isolate this responsibility. Logically, the task should be done by the study director and the participating scientists working in concert with the QAU and laboratory management. It can be covered by an SOP.

Subpart C – Facilities

Section 58.41 General.

No questions were asked on the subject.

Section 58.43 Animal Care Facilities.

1. Do the GLPs require clean/dirty separation for the animal care areas?

   No. They do require adequate separation of species and studies.

2. Do the GLPs require that separate animal rooms be used to house test systems and conduct different studies?

   No. The GLPs require separate areas adequate to assure proper separation of test systems, isolation of individual projects, animal quarantine and routine or specialized housing of animals, as necessary to achieve the study objectives.

3. Do the GLPs require that access to animal rooms be limited only to authorized individuals?

   No. However, undo stresses and potentially adverse influences on the test system should be minimized.

Section 58.45 Animal Supply Facilities.

No questions were asked on the subject.

Section 58.47 Facilities for Handling Test and Control Articles.

1. Do test and control articles have to be maintained in locked storage units?

   No, but accurate records of test and control article accountability must be maintained.

Section 58.49 Laboratory operation areas.

No questions were asked on the subject.

Section 58.51 Specimen and data storage facilities.

1. What do the GLPs require with regard to facilities for the archives?

    Space should be provided for archives limited to access by authorized personnel. Storage conditions should minimize deterioration of documents and specimens.

Section 58.53 Administrative and personnel facilities.

No questions were asked on the subject.

Subpart D – Equipment

Section 58.61 Equipment design.

No questions were asked on the subject.

Section 58.63 Maintenance and calibration of equipment.

1. Has FDA established guidelines for the frequency of calibration of equipment (balances) used in nonclinical laboratory studies?

    The agency has not established guidelines for the frequency of calibration of balances used in nonclinical laboratory studies. This would be a large undertaking in part due to the wide variety of equipment that is available and to the differing workloads that would be imposed on the equipment. It is suggested that you work with the equipment manufacturers and your study directors to arrive at a suitable calibration schedule. The key point is that the calibration should be frequent enough to assure data validity. The maintenance and calibration schedules should be part of the SOPs for each instrument.

2. When an equipment manufacturer performs the routine equipment maintenance, do the equipment manufacturer's maintenance procedures have to be described in the facilities' SOPs?

    No. The facilities' SOPs would have to state that maintenance was being performed by the equipment manufacturer according to their own procedures.

Subpart E – Testing Facilities Operation

Section 58.81 Standard Operating Procedures.

1. What amount of detail should be included in the standard operating procedures (SOPs)?

> The GLPs do not specify the amount of detail to be included in the SOPs. The SOPs are intended to minimize the introduction of systematic error into a study by ensuring that all personnel will be familiar with and use the same procedures. The adequacy of the SOPs is a key responsibility of management. A guideline of adequacy that could be used is to determine whether the SOPs are understood and can be followed by trained laboratory personnel.

2. Can the study director authorize changes in the SOPS?

> No. Approval of the SOPS and changes thereto is a function of laboratory management.

3. How many copies of the complete laboratory SOPS are needed?

> Each workstation should have access to the SOPS applicable to the work performed at the station. A complete set of the SOPS, including authorized amendments, should be maintained in the archives.

4. Who approves the SOPS of the Quality Assurance Unit?

> Laboratory Management.

5. To what extent are computer programs to be documented as SOPS?

> The GLPs do not specify the contents of individual SOPS, but the SOP that deals with computerized data acquisition should include the purpose of the program, the specifications, the procedures, the end products, the language, the interactions with other programs, procedures for assuring authorized data entry and access, procedures for making and authorizing changes to the program, the source listing of the program and perhaps even a flow chart. The laboratory's computer specialists should determine what other characteristics need to be described in the SOP.

Q&A

Section 58.83 Reagents and solutions.

1. What are the GLP requirements for labeling of reagents purchased directly from manufacturers?

    All reagents used in a nonclinical laboratory have to be labeled to indicate identity, titer or concentration, storage requirements, and expiration date. Purchased reagents usually carry all these items except for the expiration date, so the laboratory should label the reagent containers with an expiration date. The expiration date selected should be in line with laboratory experience and need not require specific stability testing.

2. How extensive should the procedures be for confirming the quality of incoming reagents used in nonclinical laboratory studies?

    Laboratory management should make this decision but the SOPS should document the actual procedures used.

3. Do the procedures used for preparing the S9 activator fraction (liver microsomal challenge to be performed in accord with the GLPs?

    No. The GLPs consider the S9 activator fraction to be a reagent. Therefore, it must be labeled properly, stored properly, tested prior to use in accord with adequate SOPs, and it can not be used if its potency is below established specifications.

4. Do the GLPs require the use of product accountability procedures for reagents and chemicals used in a nonclinical laboratory study?

    No.

Section 58.90 Animal care.

1. Can diseased animals received from a supplier be diagnosed, treated, certified "well" and then entered into a nonclinical laboratory study?

    The GLPs provide for this procedure by including provisions directed towards animal quarantine and isolation. The question of whether such animals can be entered into a study, however, is a scientific one that should be answered by the veterinarian-in-charge and the study director and other scientists involved in the study.

2. Do the GLPs prohibit the use of primates for multiple nonclinical laboratory studies?

    No. Again, the question is a scientific one and the potential impact of multiple use on study interpretation should be carefully assessed.

3. Is a photocopy of an animal purchase order, which has been signed and dated by the individual receiving the shipment sufficient proof of animal receipt?

    Yes, but actual shipping tickets are also acceptable.

4. Does FDA have guidelines for animal bedding?

    No, but the GLPs prohibit the use of bedding which can interfere with the objectives of the study.

5. Does FDA permit the sterilization of animal feed with ethylene oxide?

    No.

6. For certain test systems (timed-pregnant rodents), it is not possible to use long quarantine periods. Do the GLPs specify quarantine periods for each test system?

    No. The quarantine period can be established by the veterinarian in charge of animal care and should be of sufficient length to permit evaluation of health status.

7. How are feed and water contaminants to be dealt with?

    The protocol should include a positive statement as to the need for conducting feed analysis for contaminants. If analysis is necessary, the identities and specifications for the contaminants should be listed. The need for analysis as well as the specifications should be determined by the study scientists. Water contaminants can be handled similarly.

8. How is the adequacy of bedding materials to be handled?

    This can be handled, as are the analyses for possible contaminants in feed and water. The study director and

Q&A

associated scientists should consider the bedding and its possible impact on the study. The results of this consideration should appear in the protocol.

9. What do the GLPs require in regard to assuring the genetic quality of animals used in a nonclinical laboratory study?

This is a scientific issue that is not specifically addressed by the GLPs. Suitability of the test system for use in a study is a protocol matter and any required testing procedure should be arrived at by the study scientists.

10. Do the GLPs require specific procedures for the microbiological monitoring of animals used in nonclinical laboratory studies?

The procedures used should be in accord with acceptable veterinary medical practice.

11. The Japanese are preparing animal care guidelines, which are similar but not identical to the U.S. guidelines prepared by NIH. Would these be acceptable?

Japanese guidelines that are similar, but no less stringent, in the important particulars with the NIH guidelines would be acceptable to FDA.

12. What is the frequency of feed contaminant analysis?

If contaminant analyses are required by the protocol, then the GLPs require periodic analysis of the feed to ensure that the contaminant level is at or below that judged to be acceptable. Statistical procedures should be used to determine the frequency of analysis since this is dependent on the specific chemical characteristics of the interfering contaminant.

13. It is necessary to use "official" methods of analysis to determine the levels of interfering contaminants?

No. The methods should be appropriate for the analysis and FDA reserves the right to examine the raw data supporting the analytical results.

14. Do the GLPs require production facilities to be dedicated to the manufacture of specific animal feeds used in nonclinical laboratory studies?

No.

15. Is a separate room required for animal necropsy?

> No. The GLPs require separate areas and/or rooms as necessary to prevent any activity from having an adverse effect on the study. If the necropsy is done in an animal room, precautions should be taken to minimize disturbances that may interfere with the study.

Subpart F – Test and Control Articles

Section 58.105 Test and control article characterization.

1. Is it necessary to retain samples of feed from nonclinical laboratory studies in which the feed serves as the control article?

> Yes. It is not necessary; however, to retain reserve samples of feed from studies that involves test article administration by routes other than feed.

2. What expiration date is placed on the label of test articles whose stability is being assessed concurrently with the conduct of the study?

> In this situation, the stability of the test article is unknown, but periodic analysis data exist. The label should contain a statement such as "see protocol" or "see periodic analysis results" so that test article users will know that current analytical data should be examined prior to continued use of the test article.

3. If analysis of the reserve samples is required by the Study Director or the QAU, is it permitted?

> Yes, but sufficient reserve sample should be retained so that the sample is not exhausted.

4. Are physical and chemical tests conducted on test articles required to be done under the GLPs?

> According to section 58.105, such tests conducted to characterize the specific batch of test article used in the nonclinical laboratory study are covered.

Q&A

Section 58.107 Test and control article handling.

1. With regard to safety studies in large animals (cattle, horses, etc.), must test article accountability be maintained and can the animals be used-for food purposes?

   Test article accountability must be maintained. For guidance on whether the treated animals can be used for food, you should contact the appropriate individuals in the Center for Veterinary Medicine.

Section 58.113 Mixtures of articles with carriers.

1. Do the GLPs require tests for homogeneity, concentration, and stability on mixtures of control articles used as positive controls?

   Yes.

2. Do test or control article concentration assays have to be performed on each batch of test or control article carrier mixture?

   No. The GLPs require only periodic analysis of test or control article carrier mixtures.

3. What is the purpose of periodic analysis requirement for test or control article mixtures?

   This requirement provides additional assurance that the test system is being exposed to protocol-specified quantities of test article. Whereas, in most instances proper assurance is obtained through adequate uniformity-of-mixing studies, adequate SOPs, and trained personnel, occasionally the mixing equipment can malfunction or other uncontrollable events can occur which lead to improper dosages. These events can be recognized through periodic analysis.

4. For acute studies, does the test article carrier mixture have to be analyzed (single dose studies)?

   Yes, but the analysis need not be done prior to the study provided the mixture is stable in storage.

5. For liquid dosing studies where the test article mixture is made by dilution of the highest dose, which dose should be analyzed?

> The lowest dose would be appropriate since it would confirm the efficacy of the dilution process, however the GLPs do not prohibit the analysis of any of the other doses.

6. Do homogeneity studies need to be done on solutions and suspensions of test articles used in acute nonclinical laboratory studies?

> The answers to these questions are yes for suspensions of test articles and no for true solutions of test articles.

7. The analysis of test article mixtures that are used in acute studies is problematic. Usually at the stage of product development, the analytical method is not fully developed. Also, getting the analytical department to schedule the analysis is difficult. Stability is not a problem since fresh solutions are used. In view of the fact that acute studies are not pivotal in gaining approval of a research or marketing permit, is it necessary to analyze test article mixtures?

> Yes. Although acute studies may be of lesser importance in assessing the safety of human drugs, they are important for animal drugs, biological products and certain food additives. For this reason, there must be some assurance that the test system was dosed with protocol specified quantities of test article. The GLPs do not require that the analysis be done prior to the use of the test article mixture provided that the mixture is stable on storage.

Subpart G – Protocol for the Conduct of A Nonclinical Laboratory Study

Section 58.120 Protocol.

1. What are the proposed starting and completion dates for a nonclinical laboratory study?

> There is a good deal of confusion on these dates and proper interpretation impacts on several GLP areas. Accordingly, the following clarification is offered: At the time of protocol development, the study director is to propose to management the approximate time frame of the study. Section

58.120(a)(4), therefore, requires that the protocol contain the proposed starting and completion date of the study. These dates are somewhat discretionary provided that they are identified in the protocol. Suitable identification can be the date of first dosing of the test system to the date of last dosing, the date of allocation of the test system to the experimental units to the date of necropsy of the last animal on test, the date of receipt of the test system to the date of final histopathological examination, or any combination of these or any other logical starting and completion dates. After this, the protocol is signed by the study director and forwarded for approval to management. Management approves, if indicated, signs and dates and at this point the study becomes a regulated study and must be entered on the Master Schedule Sheet. The study is carried on the Master Schedule Sheet until the study director submits a signed and dated final report. Thus, for Master Schedule Sheet purposes, the starting date of the study is the date of protocol approval by management and the completion date of the study is the date of signature of the final report by the study director. Neither of the foregoing timeframes need be used to define the study terms described in section 58.35(b)(3) and section 58.105(d). For these sections, the traditional terms found in the toxicology literature may be used.

2. Must an analytical method be totally contained in the protocol?

No. The protocol must state the type and frequency of tests to be made. Type can be connoted by reference to literature citations or the SOPs as applicable.

3. Does each nonclinical laboratory study require a sponsor-approved specific protocol?

Yes. However, the laboratory that conducts the study can also qualify as the sponsor of the study.

4. Do unforeseen circumstances which occur during a study and which necessitate minor operational changes have to be reported as protocol amendments?

Unforeseen circumstances, which have only a one-time effect (different date of sample collection, animal weighings) need to be reported only in the raw data and the final report. However, such circumstances, which result in a systematic change, e.g. in the SOPS or in the protocol, should also be made by a protocol amendment. The protocol amendment need not be made in advance but should be made as rapidly as possible.

5. Pathologists at a firm would like to take tissues from animals in a nonclinical study, which would be used to conduct exploratory research studies. The tissues would not be part of the nonclinical laboratory study design and the results would not necessarily pertain to the study objectives. What would the GLPs require in this case?

    The protocol should state that tissues are to be taken from the experimental animals and that the tissues would be used for exploratory research purposes. If any effects were observed in the exploratory research studies, which would influence the interpretation of the results of the nonclinical laboratory study, these effects must be reported in the final report.

6. Does the protocol have to list the SOPS used in a specific study?

    The protocol must list the type and frequency of tests, analyses, and measurements to be made in the study. Where these are covered by SOPS, they should be listed in the protocol.

7. Do the GLPs require that absorption studies be done on each test article?

    No. The GLPs require that, if absorption studies are needed to achieve the scientific objectives of the study plan, the protocol should describe the methods to be used to determine absorption. Whether or not absorption studies are required is a scientific issue to be decided by the study scientists.

8. Who assesses protocol validity (Number of animals, test article dosage, test system, etc.)?

    This is done by the study scientists using the scientific literature, published guidelines, advice from regulatory agencies, and prior experimental work.

Q&A

Section 58.130 Conduct of a nonclinical laboratory study.

1. Does raw data collected in nonclinical laboratory studies have to be cosigned by a second individual?

    No.

2. What are the GLP requirements that are applicable to computerized data - acquisition systems?

    An acceptable system must satisfy the following criteria:

    a. Only authorized individuals can make data entries,

    b. data entries may not be deleted, but changes may be made in the form of dated amendments which provide the reason for data change,

    c. the data base must be made as tamperproof as possible,

    d. the SOPs should describe the procedures used for ensuring the validity of the data, and

    e. either the magnetic media or hardcopy printouts are considered to be raw data.

3. In Japan, employees do not sign raw data records but rather they use an official seal, which is unique to the employee. Is this an acceptable procedure?

    Yes.

4. Do tissue slides have to carry the complete sample labeling information stated in the GLPs?

    No, accession numbers are permitted providing that these numbers can be translated into the information required under Section 58.130(c).

5. Is a positive notation (a statement of what was done in the raw data) required for routine laboratory operations such as:

    a. identifying animals,

    b. shaving or abrading rabbits,

c. specific dosing procedures, and

d. fasting of animals?

Yes.

6. Do the GLPs require the entry of raw data into bound notebooks?

No.

7. Is it acceptable to manually transcribe raw data into notebooks if it is verified accurate by signature and date?

Technically the GLPs do not preclude such an approach. It is not a preferred procedure, however, since the chance of transcription errors would exist. Accordingly, such an approach should be used only when necessary and in this event the raw data should also be retained.

Subpart J – Records and Reports

Section 58.185 Reporting of nonclinical laboratory study results.

1. Do contributing scientist's reports have to be prepared and appended to final reports or can the contributing scientist's report be included in the final report prepared by the study director and signed by each contributing scientist?

The signed reports of contributing scientists should be appended to the final report.

2. Does Section 58:115(a) describe the format for submission of a final report?

The cited section describes the information that has to be submitted in a final report but the specific format is left up to the laboratory.

3. Do all circumstances that may have affected the quality of the data have to be described in the final report?

Yes.

4. Who approves the final report of a nonclinical laboratory study?

> The GLPs do not address the issue of approval of the final report. According to the GLPs, the final report is official when it is signed and dated by the study director. If persons reviewing the final report request changes, then such changes must be made by way of a formal amendment.

5. Can the chemistry information required by Section 58.185(a)(4) be located elsewhere in the application for a research or marketing permit?

> Yes. The final report should, however, reference the location of the chemistry information.

6. Does everyone who participated in a study have to be identified in the final report?

> No. The final report need identify only the name of the study director, the names of other participating scientists, and the names of all supervisory personnel.

7. Does the phase of the study, which has been inspected, need to be identified in the QAU statement in the final report?

> No.

8. How are protocol deviations, which are discovered after the completion of the study to be handled?

> The deviations should be described in the final report and in the study records.

9. How does the agency view interim reports of nonclinical laboratory studies?

> Interim reports are to be treated the same as final reports, i.e., they are to be reviewed by the QAU so that the summarized data accurately reflects the raw data.

Section 58.190 Storage and retrieval of records and data.

1. Certain raw data records are not study specific (pest control, instrument calibration). Must these be filed in the archives in each study file?

   No. These can be filed in a retrievable fashion such as chronological in the archives

2. Where should the QAU records be retained?

   At the completion of a study, QAU records and inspection reports should be retained in the archives.

3. At the termination of a nonclinical laboratory study, can a contractor send all of the raw data, study records, and specimens to the sponsor of the study?

   The regulations do not specifically address this issue. Section 58.195(g) requires contract laboratories that go out of business to transfer all raw data and records to the sponsor. Likewise, Section 58.190(b) permits raw data and study records to be stored elsewhere (other than the contract laboratory location) provided that the contract laboratory's archives have reference to the other locations and provided that the final study report identifies the other locations as directed by Section 58.195(a)(13).

   Consequently, it is permissible for the sponsor to retain all raw data and records from the date of termination of the nonclinical laboratory study. Common sense dictates, however, that the contract laboratory keep copies of the material that has been forwarded to the sponsor.

4. Can a study director or a pathologist be responsible for storing and retaining specimens and raw data?

   Yes, the GLPs permit multiple archival locations provided that these locations are identified in the central archives and that they provide adequate storage conditions and authorized access features.

Section 58.195 Retention of records.

1. With regard to blood and urine specimens, which are analyzed for both labile and stable constituents, is it necessary to retain the specimen until the most stable constituent deteriorates?

    All specimens should be retained for the term required by the regulations or for as long as their quality permits meaningful reevaluation, whichever is shorter.

2. For a GLP regulated metabolism study, whole tissues are homogenized and aliquots thereof are used for analysis. Is it necessary to retain all of the remaining homogenate as a reserve sample?

    No, it is only necessary to retain a representative sample large enough to repeat the original measurements.

3. If animals used in acute studies are subjected to necropsy, is it necessary to retain the organs as study specimens.

    Yes.

Conforming Amendments

1. Do acute studies not done in conformity with the GLPs have to be identified in the conforming amendment statement?

    Yes.

2. How extensive should the conforming amendment statement be for preliminary exploratory studies that are exempt from GLP coverage?

    The statement should be brief and indicate the GLP-exempt status of the study.

3. For contracted nonclinical laboratory studies, who is responsible for preparing the GLP compliance statement required by the conforming amendments?

    The preparation of the conforming amendment statement is the responsibility of the product sponsor and the statement should be submitted as part of the application for a research or marketing permit. The contractor, however, should identify for the sponsor those non-GLP practices, which were used in each nonclinical laboratory study so that a proper conforming amendment statement can be prepared.

4. Who signs the conforming amendment statement?

This can be the same individual in the firm who signs the official application for a research or marketing permit.

5. Is a specific conforming amendment statement as required by Part 314(f)(7) to be prepared for each nonclinical laboratory study?

Yes. GLP deviations have to be identified for all nonclinical laboratory studies. This can be done by preparing a single comprehensive statement, which includes all safety studies in the respective official filing. The conforming amendment statement in the official filing should be located in proximity to the animal safety studies section.

General

1. Have any nonclinical laboratories been disqualified since June 20, 1979?

No.

2. Does FDA reject nonclinical laboratory studies that have not been conducted in full compliance with the GLPs?

Not necessarily. The GLP Compliance Program provides guidance on the issue. For FDA to reject a study, it is necessary to find that there were deviations from the GLPs and that these deviations were of such a nature as to compromise the quality and integrity of the study covered by the agency inspection.

Q&A

3. Must copies of the SOPs be submitted along with an application for a research or marketing permit?

No.

4. What should be done about nonclinical laboratory studies that are stopped prior to completion?

The agency recognizes that a variety of circumstances *(disease outbreak, power failures, etc.) can lead to the premature -termination of a nonclinical laboratory study. In these cases, a short final report should be prepared that describes the reasons for study termination.

5. Has the agency established permissible limits for environmental controls (temperature, humidity and lighting) for the animal facilities?

No, these are scientific matters that should be described in the protocol and/or the SOPs. Of course, accurate records should be maintained.

Part III

Redbook 2000

Redbook 2000: IV.B.1 General Guidelines for Designing and Conducting Toxicity Studies

November 2003

Toxicological Principles for the Safety Assessment of Food Ingredients

Redbook 2000

Chapter IV.B.1. General Guidelines for Designing and Conducting Toxicity Studies[1]

This guidance represents the Food and Drug Administration's (FDA's) current thinking on this topic. It does not create or confer any rights for or on any person and does not operate to bind FDA or the public. You can use an alternative approach if the approach satisfies the requirements of the applicable statutes and regulations. If you want to discuss an alternative approach, contact the FDA staff responsible for implementing this guidance. If you cannot identify the appropriate FDA staff, call the appropriate number listed on the title page of this guidance.

I.   Good Laboratory Practice

II.   Test Animals

III.   Test Substance

IV.   Experimental Design

V.   Observations and Clinical Tests

VI.   Necropsy and Microscopic Examination

VII.   References

---

[1] Available on the FDA website at: http://www.fda.gov/Food/ GuidanceComplianceRegulatoryInformation/GuidanceDocuments/FoodIngredien tsandPackaging/Redbook/ucm078315.htm

General Guidelines for Toxicity Studies

Guidelines that are common to several or all toxicity studies are described in this section. Guidelines for specific recommended toxicity studies are found in Chapter IV.C., including: genetic toxicity studies (Chapter IV.C.1.), acute oral toxicity studies (Chapter IV.C.2. in the 1993 draft "Redbook II"), short-term toxicity studies with rodents and non-rodents (Chapter IV.C.3.a. and b., respectively), subchronic toxicity studies with rodents and non-rodents (Chapter IV.C.4.a. and b., respectively), one-year toxicity studies with non-rodents (Chapter IV.C.5.), carcinogenicity studies with rodents (Chapter IV.C.6. in the 1993 draft "Redbook II"), combined chronic toxicity/carcinogenicity studies with rodents (Chapter IV.C.7. in the 1993 draft "Redbook II"), in utero exposure phase for addition to rodent toxicity studies (Chapter IV.C.8. in the 1993 draft "Redbook II"), reproduction and developmental toxicity studies (Chapter IV.C.9.a. and b., respectively), and neurotoxicity studies (Chapter IV.C.10.). We encourage sponsors/submitters of petitions/notifications to also become familiar with the Guidance for Reporting Results of Toxicity Studies (Chapter IV.B.2.), Pathology Considerations in Toxicity Studies (Chapter IV.B.3.), and Statistical Considerations in Toxicity Studies (Chapter IV.B.4.) during the development of study design.

Scientifically justified changes to this section of the 1993 draft "Redbook II" have been made following consultation with other authoritative guidelines and publications.[2, 3, 4, 5, 6, 7, 8, 9]

---

[2] EPA Health Effects Test Guidelines OPPTS 870.3050, 28-Day Oral Toxicity in Rodents, July 2000

[3] EPA Health Effects Test Guidelines OPPTS 870.3150, 90-Day Oral Toxicity in Non-Rodents, August 1998

[4] EPA Health Effects Test Guidelines OPPTS 870.3100, 90-Day Oral Toxicity in Rodents, August 1998

[5] EPA Health Effects Test Guidelines OPPTS 870.4100, Chronic Toxicity, August 1998

[6] 5.OECD Guideline For The Testing Of Chemicals , Repeated Dose 90-day Oral Toxicity Study in Non-Rodents, 409, September 1998

[7] 6.OECD Guideline For The Testing Of Chemicals , Repeated Dose 90-day Oral Toxicity Study in Rodents, 408, September 1998

[8] 7.OECD Guideline For The Testing Of Chemicals , Repeated Dose 28-day Oral Toxicity Study in Rodents, 407, July 1995

[9] 8.Kurt Weingand et al., 1996. "Harmonization of Animal Clinical Pathology Testing in Toxicity and Safety Studies", Fundamental and Applied Toxicology, 29, pp 198-201.

I. Good Laboratory Practice

Nonclinical laboratory studies must be conducted according to U.S. FDA good laboratory practice (GLP) regulations, issued under Part 58. Title 21. Code of Federal Regulations. This document may be obtained from the Superintendent of Documents, U.S. Government Printing Office, Washington, D.C., 20402, (toll free 866-512-1800).

II. Test Animals

A. Care, Maintenance and Housing:

Recommendations about the care, maintenance, and housing of animals contained in NIH publication 85-23, "Guide for the Care and Use of Laboratory Animals"[10], and the DHEW publication no. 78-23 should be followed unless they conflict with specific recommendations in these guidelines.

B. Selection of Species, Strains and Sex:

These guidelines are for studies with rodents (usually rats) and non-rodents (usually dogs); if other species are used, modifications of these guidelines may be necessary. Both male and female test animals, that are healthy and have not been subjected to previous experimental procedures should be used.

It is important to consider the test animals' general sensitivity and the responsiveness of particular organs and tissues of test animals to toxic chemicals when selecting rodent species, strains, and substrains for toxicity studies. The selection of the use of inbred, out-bred, or hybrid rodent strains for toxicity tests should be based upon the scientific questions to be answered. Additionally, it is important that test animals come from well-characterized and healthy colonies. Because recent information suggests survivability problems exist for some strains of rats, test animals should be selected that are likely to achieve the recommended duration of the study. FDA encourages petitioners and notifiers to consult with Agency scientists before toxicity testing is begun if they have questions about the appropriateness of a particular species, strain, or substrain.

IV.B.1

---

[10] National Research Council Institute of Laboratory Animal Resources. 1996. Guide for the Care and Use of Laboratory Animals. National Academy Press, Washington, DC.

C. Age:

Testing should be performed on young animals, with dosing beginning as soon as possible after weaning and following an acclimation period of at least 5 days.Dosing of rodents should begin no later than 6 to 8 weeks of age. When dogs are used, dosing should begin no later than 4 to 6 months of age.

D. Number and Sex:

Equal numbers of males and females of each species and strain should be used for the study. In general, for subchronic toxicity studies, experimental and control groups should have at least 20 rodents per sex per group or at least 4 dogs per sex per group. Ten rodents/sex/group may be acceptable for subchronic rodent studies when the study is considered to be range-finding in nature or when longer term studies are anticipated. These recommendations will help ensure that the number of animals that survive until the end of the study will be sufficient to permit a meaningful evaluation of toxicological effects.

If interim necropsies are planned, the number of animals per sex per group should be increased by the number scheduled to be sacrificed before completion of the study; for rodents, at least 10 animals per sex per group should be available for interim necropsy.

E. Infected Animals:

Generally, it is not possible to treat animals for infection during the course of a study without risking interaction between the compound used for treatment and the test substance. This interaction may confound or complicate the interpretation of study results.

F. Animal Identification:

Test animals should be characterized by reference to their species, strain (and substrain), sex, age, and weight. Each animal must be assigned a unique identification number (e.g., ear tag, implanted identification chip, tatoo).

G. Caging:

Animals should be housed one per cage or run (single-caged) except during mating and lactation and for acute toxicity studies. This recommendation reflects three points of consideration:

- The amount of feed consumed by each animal in the study cannot be determined when more than one animal is housed in each cage. This information is necessary in the determination of feed efficiency (relationship of feed consumed to body weight gained).

- Minimizing the possibility of confounding analyses and determining whether decreases in body weight gain are due to decreased palatability or substance mediated toxicity.

- Organs and tissues from moribund and dead animals which are single-caged would not be lost due to cannibalism.

H. Diet:

In general, feed and water should be provided ad libitum to animals in toxicity studies, and the diets for these studies should meet the nutritional requirements of the species[11, 12, 13, 14] for normal growth and reproduction. Unless special circumstances apply which justify otherwise, care should be taken to ensure that the diets of the compound treated groups of animals are isocaloric (equivalent in caloric density) with and contain the same levels of nutrients (e.g., fiber, micronutrients) as the diets of the control group. Unrecognized or inadequately controlled dietary variables may result in nutritional imbalances or caloric deprivation that could confound interpretation of the toxicity study results (e.g., lifespan, background rates of tumor incidences) and alter the outcome and reproducibility of the studies.

The following issues are important to consider when establishing diets for animals in toxicity studies:

When the test substance has no caloric value and constitutes a substantial amount of the diet (e.g., more than 5%), both caloric and nutrient densities of the high dose diet would be diluted in comparison to the diets of the other groups. As a consequence, some high dose animals may receive higher test article doses than expected because

---

[11] Nutrient Requirements of Laboratory Animals, Fourth Revised Edition, Subcommittee on Laboratory Animal Nutrition, Committee on Animal Nutrition, Board on Agriculture, National Research Council, 1995.

[12] 11.Nutrient Requirements of Dogs, Revised, Committee on Animal Nutrition, National Research Council, 1985.

[13] 12.Nutrient Requirements of Swine: 10th Revised Edition, Subcommittee on Swine Nutrition, Committee on Animal Nutrition, National Research Council, 1998.

[14] 13.Nutrient Requirements of Rabbits, Second Revised Edition, Committee on Animal Nutrition, National Research Council, 1977.

IV.B.1

---

animals fed such diluted diets ad libitum may eat more than animals in other dosed groups to compensate for the differences in energy and nutrient content of the high dose diets. Such circumstances make it especially important that feed consumption of these animals be as closely and accurately monitored as possible in order to determine whether changes observed could be due to overt toxicity of the test substance or to a dietary imbalance. To further aid in this assessment, two control groups can be used; one group would be fed the undiluted control diet and a second group would be fed the control diet supplemented with an inert filler (e.g., methylcellulose) at a percentage equal to the highest percentage of the test substance in the diet.

When the vehicle for the test substance is expected to have caloric and/or nutritional values, which are greater than that of the control ration, an adjustment in the caloric and/or nutritional components may be necessary.

When administration of the test substance is expected to have an effect on feed intake because of its unpleasant taste or texture, paired feeding can be used to eliminate the differences in consumption between control and compound treated groups. When a paired feeding study design is to be employed, pairs of litter-mate weanling rats of the same sex and approximate size are selected and fed the control or the experimental diet. Animals should be single-caged so that feed consumption can be determined daily, and the control animal is then fed an amount of food equal to that which the paired experimental animal ate on the preceding day. If the test substance is non-nutritive and composes a significant proportion of the diet, the pair-fed control animals should be fed an amount of its feed such that it consumes a nutritionally equivalent amount of diet as the paired experimental animal. Additionally, the study should include a second group of control animals fed ad libitum to ensure that the impact on any observed experimental result is due to differences in energy or nutrient intake.

When the test substance interferes with the absorption of nutrients, leading to nutritional deficiencies or changes in nutrient ratios, this can confound assessment of the toxicological endpoints under consideration. For example, fat soluble vitamins may preferentially partition with a mineral oil or fat substitute which is largely unabsorbed, such that a potential deficiency in these vitamins may result. This potential may be eliminated by additional nutrient fortification of the feed for those groups receiving the test substance. Appropriate levels of nutrient fortification should be determined experimentally.

It may be preferable to use a semi-purified diet prepared with known amounts of well-characterized ingredients for short-term and subchronic toxicity studies because of batch to batch variations in diet composition (e.g., fiber, mineral, vitamins, isoflavones) in some of the commonly used laboratory animal chows. The use of these semi-purified diets, however, may not be advisable in long-term and reproductive studies due to inadequate historical data related to their influences on animal survival and toxicological endpoints. For example, loss of necessary but unidentified micronutrients in the semipurified diet may interfere with normal reproduction.

Related issues are discussed in the section on Diets for Toxicity Studies in Chapter IV.B.5. in the 1993 draft "Redbook II".

I. Assignment of Control and Compound Treated Animals:

Animals should be assigned to control and compound treated groups in a stratified random manner; this will help minimize bias and assure comparability of pertinent variables across compound treated and control groups (for example: mean body weights and body weight ranges). If other characteristics are used as the basis for randomization then that characterization should be described and justified.

Animals in all groups should be placed on study on the same day; if this is not possible because of the large number of animals in a study, animals may be placed on study over several days. If the latter recommendation is followed, a preselected portion of the control and experimental animals should be placed on the study each day in order to maintain concurrence.

J. Mortality:

Excessive mortality due to poor animal management is unacceptable and may be cause to repeat the study. For example, under normal circumstances, mortality in the control group should not exceed 10% in short and intermediate length (not lifetime) toxicity studies.

K. Autolysis:

Adequate animal husbandry practices should result in considerably less than 10% of animals and tissues or organs lost to a study because of autolysis. Autolysis in excess of this standard may be cause to repeat the study.

IV.B.1

L. Necropsy:

Necropsy should be performed soon after an animal is sacrificed or found dead, so that loss of tissues due to autolysis is minimized. When necropsy cannot be performed immediately, the animal should be refrigerated at a temperature that is low enough to prevent autolysis but not so low as to cause cell damage. If histopathological examination is to be conducted, tissue specimens should be taken from the animals and placed in appropriate fixatives when the necropsy is performed.

III. Test Substance

The test substance used in toxicity studies should be the same substance that the petitioner/notifier intends to market. A single lot of test substance should be used throughout the study, when possible. Alternatively, lots that are as similar as possible in purity and composition should be used.

A. Identity:

The identity of the test substance or mixture of substances to be tested should be known. We urge petitioners/notifiers to consult with the Agency in determination of test compound and to provide a Chemical Abstract Service (CAS) Registry Number or Numbers.

B. Composition/Purity:

The composition of the test substance should be known including the name and quantities of all major components, known contaminants and impurities, and the percentage of unidentifiable materials.

C. Conditions of Storage:

The test sample should be stored under conditions that maintain its stability, quality, and purity until the studies are complete.

D. Expiration Date:

The expiration date of the test material should be known and easily available. Test materials should not be used past their expiration date.

IV. Experimental Design

A. Duration of Testing:

Animals should be exposed to the test substance 7 days per week for the designated length of time of the study.

B. Route of Administration:

The route of administration of the test substance should approximate that of normal human exposure, if possible. For food ingredients (e.g., food and color additives) the oral route of administration is preferred. A justification should be provided when other routes are used. The same method of administration should be used for all test animals throughout the study.

The test substance should be administered in one of the following ways:

- **In the diet**, if human exposure to the test substance is likely to be through consumption of solid foods or a combination of solid and liquid foods. If the test substance is added to the diet, animals should not be able to selectively consume either basal diet or test substance in the diet on the basis of color, smell, or particle size. If the compound is mixed with ground feed and pelleted, nothing in the pelleting process should affect the test substance (for example, heat-labile substances may be destroyed during pellet production by a steam process). When the test substance is administered in the diet, dietary levels should be expressed as mg of the test substance per kg of feed.

- **Dissolved in the drinking water**, if the test substance is likely to be ingested in liquid form (for example, in soft drinks or beer), or if administration in the diet is inappropriate for other reasons. The amount of test substance administered in drinking water should be expressed as mg of test substance per ml of water.

- **By encapsulation or oral intubation (gavage)**, if the two previous methods are unsatisfactory or if human exposure is expected to be through daily ingestion of single, large doses instead of continual ingestion of small doses. If the test substance is administered by gavage, it should be given at approximately the same time each day. The maximum volume of solution that can be given by gavage in one dose depends on the test animal's size; for rodents, the volume ordinarily should not exceed 1 ml/100 g body weight. If the gavage vehicle is oil (see Chapter IV.B.5.b. in the

IV.B.1

1993 draft "Redbook II"), then the volume should be no more than 0.4 ml/100 g of body weight, and the use of a low-fat diet should be considered. If the test substance must be given in divided doses, all doses should be administered within a 6 hour period. Doses of test substance administered by gavage should be expressed as mg of test substance per ml of gavage vehicle. Finally, the petitioner/notifier should provide information that can allow the reviewer to conclude that administration of the test compound by encapsulation or gavage is equivalent in all toxicologically important respects to administration in the diet or drinking water. Alternatively, metabolic information on both modes of administration should be provided so that appropriate interpretation of data can be accomplished.

C. Dose groups:

Three to five dose levels of the test substance and concurrent control groups should be used with both males and females. Information obtained from acute (Chapter IV.C.2. in the 1993 draft "Redbook II") and short-term (Chapter IV.C.3.a. and b.) toxicity studies can help determine appropriate doses for subchronic studies.

1. Selection of Treatment Doses:

Dose selection for toxicity studies should be based on information related to the toxicity of the test substance.

A minimum of three dose levels of the test substance and a concurrent control group should be used in toxicity studies. When designing and conducting toxicity studies the following should be considered: 1) the high dose should be sufficiently high to induce toxic responses in test animals; 2) the low dose should not induce toxic responses in test animals; and 3) the intermediate dose should be sufficiently high to elicit minimal toxic effects in test animals (such as alterations in enzyme levels or slight decreases in body weight gains). No dose should cause an incidence of fatalities that prevents meaningful evaluation of the data. Administration of the test substance to all dose groups should be done concurrently.

2. Controls:

A concurrent control group of test animals is required. The control group in dietary studies should be fed the basal diet. Exceptions to this and other related information, including a discussion regarding pair-feeding, was provided above in section "II. Test Animals, H. Diet".

A carrier or vehicle for the test substance should be given to control animals at a volume equal to the maximum volume of carrier or vehicle given to any dosed group of animals. Sufficient toxicology information should be available on the carrier or vehicle to ensure that its use will not compromise the results of the study. If there is insufficient information about the toxic properties of the vehicle used to administer the test substance, an additional control group that is not exposed to the carrier or vehicle should be included. In all other respects, animals in the control group should be treated the same as animals in dosed groups. (See additional information in "II. Test Animals, H. Diet" above.)

D. Computerized systems

Computerized systems that are used in the generation, measurement, or assessment of data should be developed, validated, operated, and maintained in ways that are compliant with Good Laboratory Practice principles.[15]

V. Observations and Clinical Tests

A. Observations of Test Animals:

Routine cage-side observations should be made on all animals at least once or twice a day throughout the study for general signs of pharmacologic and toxicologic effects, morbidity and mortality. The usual interval between observations should be at least 6 hours. Individual records should be maintained for each animal and the time of onset and the characteristics and progression of any effects should be recorded, preferably using a scoring system.

An expanded set of clinical evaluations, performed inside and outside of the cage, should be carried out in short-term and subchronic toxicity studies in rodents and non-rodents, in one-year non-rodent toxicity studies, and reproductive toxicity studies in rodents to enable detection not only of general pharmacologic and toxicologic effects but also of neurologic disorders, behavioral changes, autonomic dysfunctions, and other signs of nervous system toxicity. Specific information about the systematic clinical tests/observations is contained in Chapter IV.C.10. This expanded set of clinical

IV.B.1

---

[15] The Application of the Principles of GLP to Computerised Systems, Organisation for Economic Cooperation and Development (OECD), Environmental Monograph No. 116, Paris, 1995.

examinations (Chapter IV.C.10.), conducted inside and outside the cage, should be age appropriate and performed on all animals at least once prior to initiation of treatment, and periodically during treatment. Signs noted should include, but not be limited to, changes in skin, fur, eyes, mucous membranes, occurrence of secretions and excretions and autonomic activity (e.g., lacrimation, pilorection, pupil size, unusual respiratory pattern). Additionally, changes in gait, posture and response to handling, as well as the presence of clonic or tonic movements, stereotypes (e.g., excessive grooming, repetitive circling) or bizarre behavior (e.g., self-mutilating, walking backwards) should be recorded. Tumor development, particularly in long-term studies, should be followed: the time of onset, location, dimensions, appearance and progression of each grossly visible or palpable tumor should be recorded. During the course of a study, toxic and pharmacologic signs may suggest the need for additional clinical tests or expanded post-mortem examinations.

B. Body Weight and Feed Intake Data:

Recommendations are described in guidelines for specific toxicity study types (see Chapter IV.C. of the 1993 draft "Redbook II" and/or "Redbook 2000"). Feed spillage should be noted and adjustments made in related calculations and appropriate discussion presented in the study report.

C. Clinical Testing:

Ophthalmological examination, hematology profiles, clinical chemistry tests, and urinalyses should be performed as described in the following sections:

1. **Opthalmological Examination**: This examination should be performed by a qualified individual on all animals before the study begins and on control and high-dose animals at the end of the study. If the results of examinations at termination indicate that changes in the eyes may be associated with administration of the test substance, ophthalmological examinations should be performed on all animals in the study.

2. **Hematology**: The recommended number of animals and time intervals for hematology assessment are found in individual toxicity study guidelines (see Chapter IV.C.3.-5. of "Redbook 2000" and Chapter IV.C.2. and 6.-8. of the 1993 draft "Redbook II"). Ideally, the same rodents should be sampled at each collection time point. Blood samples should be analyzed

individually, and not pooled. If animals are sampled on more than one day during a study, blood should be drawn at approximately the same time each sampling day.

1. The following determinations are recommended:

    1. hematocrit

    2. hemoglobin concentration

    3. erythrocyte count

    4. total and differential leukocyte counts

    5. mean corpuscular hemoglobin

    6. mean corpuscular volume

    7. mean corpuscular hemoglobin concentration

    8. and a measure of clotting potential (such as clotting time, prothrombin time, thromboplastin time, or platelet count).

Test compounds may have an effect on the hematopoietic system and therefore appropriate measures should be employed so that evaluations of reticulocyte counts and bone marrow cytology may be performed if warranted. Reticulocyte counts should be obtained for each animal using automated reticulocyte counting capabilities, or from air-dried blood smears. Bone marrow slides should be prepared from each animal for evaluating bone marrow cytology. These slides would only need to be examined microscopically if effects on the hematopoietic system were noted.

3. **Clinical Chemistry**: The recommended number of animals and time intervals for clinical chemistry assessment are found in individual toxicity guidelines (see Chapter IV.C.3.-5. of "Redbook 2000" and Chapter IV.C.2. and 6.-8. of the 1993 draft "Redbook II"). Ideally, the same rodents should be sampled at each collection time point. Blood samples should be drawn at the end of the fasting time and before feeding. Fasting duration should be appropriate for the species and the analytical tests to be performed. Blood samples should be analyzed individually, and not pooled. If animals are sampled on more than one day during a study, blood should he drawn at approximately the same time each sampling day.

IV.B.1

Clinical chemistry tests that are appropriate for all test substances include measurements of electrolyte balance, carbohydrate metabolism, and liver and kidney function. Specific determinations should include:

1. Hepatocellular evaluation: select at least 3 of the following 5

    1. alanine aminotransferase (SGPT, ALT)

    2. aspartate aminotransferase (SGOT, AST)

    3. sorbitol dehydrogenase

    4. glutamate dehydrogenase

    5. total bile acids

2. Hepatobiliary evaluation: select at least 3 of the following 5

    1. alkaline phosphatase

    2. bilirubin (total)

    3. gamma-glutamyl transpeptidase (GG transferase)

    4. 5' nucleotidase

    5. total bile acids

3. Other markers of cell changes or cellular function

    1. albumin

    2. calcium

    3. chloride

    4. cholestrol(total)

    5. cholinesterase

    6. creatinine

    7. globulin (calculated)

    8. glucose (in fasted animals)

    9. phosphorous

    10. potassium

    11. protein (total)

    12. sodium

    13. triglycerides (fasting)

14. urea nitrogen

1. However, when adequate volumes of blood cannot be obtained from test animals, the following determinations should generally be given priority. FDA understands that the specific nature of the test compound may warrant the consideration of alternative tests. Appropriate justification for alternative tests should be presented in study reports.

    1. alanine aminotransferase

    2. alkaline phosphatase

    3. chloride

    4. creatinine

    5. gamma-glutamyl transpeptidase (GG transferase)

    6. glucose (in fasted animals)

    7. potassium

    8. protein (total)

    9. sodium

    10. urea nitrogen

Additional clinical chemistry tests may be recommended to extend the search for toxic effects attributable to a test substance. The selection of specific tests will be influenced by observations on the mechanism of action of the test substance. Clinical chemistry determinations that may be recommended to ensure adequate toxicological evaluation of the test substance include analyses of acid/base balance, hormones, lipids, methemoglobin, and proteins.

In spite of standard operating procedures and equipment calibration, it is not unusual to observe considerable variation in the results of clinical chemistry analyses from day to day.[16] Ideally, clinical chemistry analyses for all dose groups should be completed during one day. If this is not possible, analyses should be conducted in such a way as to minimize potential variability.

IV.B.1

---

[16] Gaylor, D.W., Suber, R.L., Wolff, G.L. and Crowell, J.A. (1987) Statistical variation of selected clinical pathological and biochemical measurements in rodents (42555) Proc. Soc. Exp. Biol. Med. , 185:361-367

4. **Urinalyses**: Timed urine volume collection should be conducted during the last week of the study and at other time intervals described in specific individual toxicity study guidelines (Chapter IV.C.3.-5. of "Redbook 2000" and Chapter IV.C.2. and 6.-8. of the 1993 draft "Redbook II"). The volume of urine collected, specific gravity, pH, glucose, and protein should be determined as well as conducting a microscopic evaluation of urine for sediment and presence of blood/blood cells.[17]

5. **Neurotoxicity Screening/Testing** : Screening for neurotoxic effects should be routinely carried out in short-term and subchronic toxicity studies with rodents (preferably rats) and non-rodents (preferably dogs), one-year studies in non-rodents, and reproductive toxicity studies in rodents. The neurotoxicity screen should be age appropriate and would typically include: (1) specific histopathological examination of tissue samples representative of major areas of the brain, spinal cord, and peripheral nervous system (see organs and tissues listed below under VI.C. Preparation of Tissues for Microscopic Examination) and (2) a functional battery of quantifiable observations and manipulative tests selected to detect signs of neurological, behavioral, and physiological dysfunctions. This functional battery is also referred to as an expanded set of clinical evaluations and is described more fully in section V.A. Observations of Test Animals in this Chapter and in Chapter IV.C.10. Neurotoxicity Studies.

Toxicity study reports should include an assessment of the potential for the test substance to adversely affect the structural or functional integrity of the nervous system. This assessment should evaluate data from the neurotoxicity screen and other toxicity data from the study, as appropriate. Based on this assessment, the petitioner should make an explicit statement about whether or not the test substance presents a potential neurotoxic hazard and if additional neurotoxicity testing is deemed appropriate. FDA recommends that additional neurotoxicity testing not be undertaken without first consulting with the Agency.

6. **Immunotoxicity**: For short-term, subchronic and developmental toxicity studies, results of clinical tests that are included in the list

---

[17] Ragan, H.A. and Weller, R.E., "Markers of Renal Function and Injury" in The Clinical Chemistry of Laboratory Animals, Second Edition 1999, Taylor & Francis, Philadelphia, PA, pp. 520-533

of primary indicators for immune toxicity (see Chapter V.C. of the 1993 draft "Redbook II") should also be evaluated as part of an immunotoxicity screen. Additional immunotoxicity tests are discussed in Chapter V.C. of the 1993 draft "Redbook II", but should not be undertaken without first consulting with the Agency.

VI. Necropsy and Microscopic Examination

A. Gross Necropsy

All test animals should be subjected to complete gross necropsy, including examination of external surfaces, orifices, cranial, thoracic and abdominal cavities, carcass, and all organs. The gross necropsy should be performed by, or under the direct supervision of, a qualified pathologist, preferably the pathologist who will later perform the microscopic examination (see below).

B. Organ Weight

Organs that should be weighed include the adrenals, brain, epididymides, heart, kidneys, liver, spleen, testes, thyroid/parathyroid, thymus, ovaries and uterus. Organs should be carefully dissected and trimmed to remove fat and other contiguous tissue and then be weighed immediately to minimize the effects of drying on organ weight.

C. Preparation of Tissues for Microscopic Examination

Generally, the following tissues should be fixed in 10% buffered formalin (or another generally recognized fixative) and sections prepared and stained with hematoxylin and eosin (or another appropriate stain) in preparation for microscopic examination. Lungs should be inflated with fixative prior to immersion in fixative. Sponsors should refer to specific studies (Chapter IV.C.1.-10.) for details.

1. adrenals

2. aorta

3. bone (femur)

4. bone marrow (sternum)

5. brain (at least 3 different levels)

IV.B.1

6. cecum

7. colon

8. corpus and cervix uteri

9. duodenum

10. epididymis

11. esophagus

12. eyes

13. gall bladder (if present)

14. Harderian gland (if present)

15. heart

16. ileum

17. jejunum

18. kidneys

19. liver

20. lung (with main-stem bronchi)

21. lymph nodes (1 related to route of administration and 1 from a distant location)

22. mammary glands

23. nasal turbinates

24. ovaries and fallopian tubes

25. pancreas

26. pituitary

27. prostate

28. rectum

29. salivary gland

30. sciatic nerve

31. seminal vesicle (if present)

32. skeletal muscle

33. skin

34. spinal cord (3 locations: cervical, mid-thoracic, lumbar)

35. spleen

36. stomach

37. testes

38. thymus (or thymic region)

39. thyroid/parathyroid

40. trachea

41. urinary bladder

42. vagina

43. Zymbal's gland (if present)

44. all tissues showing abnormality

D. Microscopic Evaluation

All gross lesions should be examined microscopically. All tissues from the animals in the control and high dose groups should be examined. If treatment related effects are noted in certain tissues, then the next lower dose level tested of those specific tissues should be examined. Successive examination of the next lower dose level continues until no effects are noted. In addition, all tissues from animals which died prematurely or were sacrificed during the study should be examined microscopically to assess any potential toxic effects.

E. Histopathology of Lymphoid Organs

Histopathological evaluation of the lymphoid organs should be performed as described in the section on immunotoxicity testing (see Chapter V.C.) for all animals in short-term and subchronic toxicity studies and developmental toxicity studies.

VII. References

1. EPA Health Effects Test Guidelines OPPTS 870.3050, 28-Day Oral Toxicity in Rodents, July 2000

2. EPA Health Effects Test Guidelines OPPTS 870.3150, 90-Day Oral Toxicity in Non-Rodents, August 1998

3. EPA Health Effects Test Guidelines OPPTS 870.3100, 90-Day Oral Toxicity in Rodents, August 1998

IV.B.1

4. EPA Health Effects Test Guidelines OPPTS 870.4100, Chronic Toxicity, August 1998

5. OECD Guideline For The Testing Of Chemicals , Repeated Dose 90-day Oral Toxicity Study in Non-Rodents, 409, September 1998

6. OECD Guideline For The Testing Of Chemicals , Repeated Dose 90-day Oral Toxicity Study in Rodents, 408, September 1998

7. OECD Guideline For The Testing Of Chemicals , Repeated Dose 28-day Oral Toxicity Study in Rodents, 407, July 1995

8. Kurt Weingand et al., 1996. "Harmonization of Animal Clinical Pathology Testing in Toxicity and Safety Studies", Fundamental and Applied Toxicology, 29, pp 198-201.

9. National Research Council Institute of Laboratory Animal Resources. 1996. Guide for the Care and Use of Laboratory Animals. National Academy Press, Washington, DC.

10. Nutrient Requirements of Laboratory Animals, Fourth Revised Edition, Subcommittee on Laboratory Animal Nutrition, Committee on Animal Nutrition, Board on Agriculture, National Research Council, 1995.

11. Nutrient Requirements of Dogs, Revised, Committee on Animal Nutrition, National Research Council, 1985.

12. Nutrient Requirements of Swine: 10th Revised Edition, Subcommittee on Swine Nutrition, Committee on Animal Nutrition, National Research Council, 1998.

13. Nutrient Requirements of Rabbits, Second Revised Edition, Committee on Animal Nutrition, National Research Council, 1977.

14. The Application of the Principles of GLP to Computerised Systems, Organisation for Economic Cooperation and Development (OECD), Environmental Monograph No. 116, Paris, 1995.

15. Gaylor, D.W., Suber, R.L., Wolff, G.L. and Crowell, J.A. (1987) Statistical variation of selected clinical pathological and

biochemical measurements in rodents (42555) Proc. Soc. Exp. Biol. Med. , 185:361-367

16. Ragan, H.A. and Weller, R.E., "Markers of Renal Function and Injury" in The Clinical Chemistry of Laboratory Animals, Second Edition 1999, Taylor & Francis, Philadelphia, PA, pp. 520-533

IV.B.1

Redbook 2000: IV.B.2 Guidelines for Reporting the Results of Toxicity Studies

November 2003

Toxicological Principles for the Safety Assessment of Food Ingredients

Redbook 2000

Chapter IV.B.2. Guidelines for Reporting the Results of Toxicity Studies[1]

This guidance represents the Food and Drug Administration's (FDA's) current thinking on this topic. It does not create or confer any rights for or on any person and does not operate to bind FDA or the public. You can use an alternative approach if the approach satisfies the requirements of the applicable statutes and regulations. If you want to discuss an alternative approach, contact the FDA staff responsible for implementing this guidance. If you cannot identify the appropriate FDA staff, call the appropriate number listed on the title page of this guidance.

Guidelines for reporting the results of toxicity studies are contained in this section. More complete information regarding Pathology and Statistics can be found in Chapters IV.B.3. and IV.B.4., respectively. The study report should include all information necessary to provide a complete and accurate description and evaluation of the study procedures and results in accordance with 21 CFR 58.185. The following sections should be included:

---

[1] Available on the FDA website at: http://www.fda.gov/Food/ GuidanceComplianceRegulatoryInformation/GuidanceDocuments/FoodIngredien tsandPackaging/Redbook/ucm078409.htm

I. Study Identification and Information

    A. Study title and report number

    B. Testing facility by name and address

    C. Duration of study

    D. Dates of:

        1. Acclimation

        2. Initiation (onset of dosing)

        3. Sacrifice/termination

        4. Study report

    E. Identification and signatures (where appropriate) of personnel primarily responsible for:

        1. Conduct of the study (i.e., study director, principal investigator)

        2. Analyses of data

        3. Histopathology

        4. Writing the report

        5. Other information contained in the report

II. Good Laboratory Practice for Nonclinical Laboratory Studies Statement

The Good Laboratory Practice (GLP) regulations were designed to establish minimal standards for conduct and reporting of nonclinical safety testing and are intended to assure the quality and integrity of safety data submitted to the FDA. Each food and color additive petition, Generally Recognized as Safe (GRAS) affirmation petition, and Food Contact Notification (FCN) must include a GLP compliance statement as set forth in 21 CFR 171.1(k), 21 CFR 71.1(g), 21 CFR 170.35(c)(1)(vi), or 21 CFR 170.101(c).

III. Quality Assurance Statement

Each study report must include a quality assurance statement signed by the quality assurance unit in accordance with 21 CFR Section

58.35(b)(7) which states: "Prepare and sign a statement to be included with the final study report which shall specify the dates inspections were made and findings reported to management and to the study director."

IV. Protocol and Amendments

A protocol for each non-clinical study should be written so that it satisfies all GLP requirements set forth in 21 CFR 58.120. The protocol should include clearly stated objectives and methods for the conduct of the study. A copy of the protocol should be attached to the study report. The study report should include statements describing all changes in or revisions of the protocol, the reasons for those changes, and any influence these changes had on the results of the study.

V. Storage, Retrieval, and Retention of Records

This section of the study report should include information regarding the availability and location of original data, specimens and samples of the test substance, in accordance with 21 CFR 58.190 and 195.

VI. Summary and Conclusions

This section of the study report should contain a brief description of:

A. Methods

B. Summary and analysis of numerical data

C. Summary and analysis of descriptive data (e.g., observations to assess neurotoxic potential)

D. The conclusions drawn from the analyses, including target organ(s) and no observed effect levels (NOELs)

The summary should highlight all significant changes in data or observations of the test substance treated groups, in comparison to the control groups, which may be an indication of toxic effects of the test substance. The summary should also include a description of the relationship between dose and the incidence/severity of lesions or abnormalities.

The summary should include a description of all circumstances that may have influenced the quality or integrity of the data or observations.

IV.B.2

VII. Test Substance

A. Identification

1. Chemical name

2. Chemical Abstracts Service (CAS) registry number (or code number)

3. Molecular structure and molecular weight

4. Qualitative and quantitative determination of its chemical composition

B. Manufacturing information

1. Lot number

2. Purity, including names and quantities of known contaminants and impurities and the percentage of unidentifiable materials

3. Expiration date

4. Stability

5. Storage instructions

C. Physical properties

1. State (i.e., powder, liquid)

2. Color

3. Solubility, in aqueous and in dosing vehicle

4. pH (pKa where applicable)

5. Boiling and melting point

D. Identification of diluents, suspending agents, emulsifiers, excipients, or other materials used in administering the test substance.

E. Sampling of test material in administered form

1. Times when sampling was performed

2. Verification of stability of test compound in administered form: method and results

   3. Verification of homogeniety of test compound in
       administered form: method and results

   4. Verification of concentration of test compound in
       administered form: method and results

F. Storage conditions: during and after the study

VIII. Test Animals

A. Species and strain (and substrain if applicable) used and,
    particularly if a strain other than a common laboratory strain is
    used in the study, rationale for selection of the strain

B. Source or supplier of the animals

C. Description of any pre-test conditioning (such as quarantine
    procedures)

D. Description of the method used to randomize animals into test
    and control groups

E. Numbers, age, and condition of animals of each sex in all test
    substance treated and control groups at the beginning and end of
    the study

F. Diet

   1. Feed

       a. Diet: lot number, composition, etc.

       b. Availability: i.e., *ad libitum*

   2. Water

       a. Availability: i.e., *ad libitum*

G. Caging conditions

   1. Number of animals per cage

   2. Bedding material

   3. Ambient temperature

   4. Humidity

   5. Lighting conditions

IV.B.2

IX. Methods

The methods section of the study report should include, but not be limited to, the following information

A. Deviations from these Redbook 2000 guidelines

    1. Describe all ways in which the test procedure deviates from these Redbook 2000 guidelines

    2. State the rationale for each deviation.

B. Experimental design and procedures (full description)

    1. Length of the study (including dates study began and ended)

    2. Data on dosage administration should include

        a. All dose levels administered, expressed as mg/kg body weight, per unit of time (e.g. day)

        b. Route of administration

        c. Method, frequency, and time of day of administration

        d. Total volume of dose plus vehicle administered to each animal, if the test substance is administered by gavage

        e. Duration of treatment period

    3. Observation of the test animals

        a. Duration of individual observation

        b. Frequency

        c. Method

    4. Sampling Conditions of specimens (hematology, clinical chemistry, urinalysis, other)

        a. Duration and time of day

        b. Frequency

        c. Method

    5. Statistical analyses: All statistical methods used should be fully described or identified by reference. For a complete discussion of the information that should be contained in this section of the study report, see Chapter IV.B.4.

XI. Results and Discussion

A. Individual animal data and results should be provided in tabular format and in sufficient detail to permit independent evaluation of the results. Describe all computerized systems used in the generation, measurement, or assessment of data including the name and version of the system (software) and the specified indications for use. The following information should be included for each test animal:

1. Time of first observation of each abnormal sign and its subsequent course. These data should be organized, when appropriate, by litter.

2. Time of death during the study. The "most probable" cause of death should also be determined and reported for those animals that were not sacrificed at the pre-scheduled time.

3. Feed and water consumption data (including feed spillage)

4. Body weights and body weight changes

5. Feed efficiency data

6. Hematology, clinical chemistry, urinalysis, and other clinical findings

7. Results of neurotoxicity and immunotoxicity studies, as appropriate

8. Gross necropsy findings including:

   a. absolute and relative organ weights

   b. description of gross lesions

   c. incidence and severity of gross lesions

9. Histopathology findings (see Chapter IV.B.3.) including:

   a. description of microscopic lesions

   b. incidence and severity of microscopic lesions

B. Summarized data from individual animals should be organized by sex and dose group and provided in tabular format. When appropriate, data should also be organized by litter. When numerical means are presented, they should be accompanied by an appropriate measure of variability, such as the standard error. For each summarized parameter, the following information should be included:

IV.B.2

1. The number of animals at the beginning of the study

2. The number of animals evaluated for each parameter

3. The day of the study (e.g., day 60, at termination) when animals were evaluated for each parameter

C. All numerical results should be evaluated by an appropriate statistical method. Refer to Chapter IV.B.4. for detailed guidelines about statistical considerations in toxicity studies.

D. Evaluation of the results should include at a minimum:

1. Discussion about the nature of relationships, if any, between exposure to the test substance and the incidence and severity of all general and specific adverse effects (such as neoplastic and non-neoplastic lesions, organ weight effects, and mortality effects), and identification of target organs.

2. Discussion about the relationship between clinical observations made during the course of a study and post mortem findings.

3. A conclusion statement regarding the dosage level at which no effects attributable to the test substance were observed (NOEL), and a discussion of any complex and/or any controversial issues surrounding that determination.

X. References

This section of the study report should include appropriate literature citations or references, for the following:

A. Test procedures

B. Statistical and other methods used to analyze the data

C. Compilation and evaluation of results

D. The basis upon which conclusions were reached

The above guidance document supersedes the previous version dated October, 2001.

Part IV

Combined Glossary and Index

Combined Glossary

505(b)(2) Application means an application submitted under section 505(b)(1) of the act for a drug for which the investigations described in section 505(b)(1)(A) of the act and relied upon by the applicant for approval of the application were not conducted by or for the applicant and for which the applicant has not obtained a right of reference or use from the person by or for whom the investigations were conducted. [21 CFR § 314]

A

Abbreviated application means the application described under 314.94, including all amendments and supplements to the application. "Abbreviated application" applies to both an abbreviated new drug application and an abbreviated antibiotic application. [21 CFR § 314]

Acceptance criteria means the product specifications and acceptance/rejection criteria, such as acceptable quality level and unacceptable quality level, with an associated sampling plan, that are necessary for making a decision to accept or reject a lot or batch (or any other convenient subgroups of manufactured units). [21 CFR § 210]

Act means the Federal Food, Drug, and Cosmetic Act (secs. 201-903 (21 U.S.C. 321-393)). [21 CFR § 11]

> *Act* means the Federal Food, Drug, and Cosmetic Act, as amended (secs. 201-902, 52 Stat. 1040et seq. as amended (21 U.S.C. 321-392)). [21 CFR § 50, § 56, § 58, § 312, § 812]

> *Act* means the Federal Food, Drug, and Cosmetic Act, as amended (21 U.S.C. 301et seq.). [21 CFR § 210]

> *Act* means the Federal Food, Drug, and Cosmetic Act (sections 201-901 (21 U.S.C. 301-392)). [21 CFR § 314]

Act means the Federal Food, Drug, and Cosmetic Act (sections 201-902, 52 Stat. 1040 et seq., as amended (21 U.S.C. 321-392)). [21 CFR § 814]

Active ingredient means any component that is intended to furnish pharmacological activity or other direct effect in the diagnosis, cure, mitigation, treatment, or prevention of disease, or to affect the structure or any function of the body of man or other animals. The term includes those components that may undergo chemical change in the manufacture of the drug product and be present in the drug product in a modified form intended to furnish the specified activity or effect. [21 CFR § 210]

Actual yield means the quantity that is actually produced at any appropriate phase of manufacture, processing, or packing of a particular drug product.

Adverse drug experience is any adverse event associated with the use of a new animal drug, whether or not considered to be drug related, and whether or not the new animal drug was used in accordance with the approved labeling (i.e., used according to label directions or used in an extralabel manner, including but not limited to different route of administration, different species, different indications, or other than labeled dosage). Adverse drug experience includes, but is not limited to: [21 CFR § 514]

(1) An adverse event occurring in animals in the course of the use of an animal drug product by a veterinarian or by a livestock producer or other animal owner or caretaker.

(2) Failure of a new animal drug to produce its expected pharmacological or clinical effect (lack of expected effectiveness).

(3) An adverse event occurring in humans from exposure during manufacture, testing, handling, or use of a new animal drug.

Agency means the Food and Drug Administration. [21 CFR § 11]

ANADA is an abbreviated new animal drug application including all amendments and supplements. [21 CFR § 514]

Applicant means the party who submits a marketing application to FDA for approval of a drug, device, or biologic product. The applicant is responsible for submitting the appropriate certification and disclosure statements required in this part. [21 CFR § 54]

Applicant means any person who submits an application or abbreviated application or an amendment or supplement to them under this part to obtain FDA approval of a new drug or an antibiotic drug and any person who owns an approved application or abbreviated application. [21 CFR § 314]

Applicant is a person or entity who owns or holds on behalf of the owner the approval for an NADA or an ANADA, and is responsible for compliance with applicable provisions of the act and regulations. [21 CFR § 514]

Application means the application described under 314.50, including all amendements and supplements to the application. [21 CFR § 314]

Application for research or marketing permit includes: [21 CFR § 50]

(1) A color additive petition, described in part 71.

(2) A food additive petition, described in parts 171 and 571.

(3) Data and information about a substance submitted as part of the procedures for establishing that the substance is generally recognized as safe for use that results or may reasonably be expected to result, directly or indirectly, in its becoming a component or otherwise affecting the characteristics of any food, described in 170.30 and 570.30.

(4) Data and information about a food additive submitted as part of the procedures for food additives permitted to be used on an interim basis pending additional study, described in 180.1.

(5) Data and information about a substance submitted as part of the procedures for establishing a tolerance for unavoidable contaminants in food and food-packaging materials, described in section 406 of the act.

(6) An investigational new drug application, described in part 312 of this chapter.

(7) A new drug application, described in part 314.

(8) Data and information about the bioavailability or bioequivalence of drugs for human use submitted as part of the procedures for issuing, amending, or repealing a bioequivalence requirement, described in part 320.

(9) Data and information about an over-the-counter drug for human use submitted as part of the procedures for classifying these drugs as generally recognized as safe and effective and not misbranded, described in part 330.

(10) Data and information about a prescription drug for human use submitted as part of the procedures for classifying these drugs as generally recognized as safe and effective and not misbranded, described in this chapter.

(11) [Reserved]

(12) An application for a biologics license, described in part 601 of this chapter.

(13) Data and information about a biological product submitted as part of the procedures for determining that licensed biological products are safe and effective and not misbranded, described in part 601.

(14) Data and information about an in vitro diagnostic product submitted as part of the procedures for establishing, amending, or repealing a standard for these products, described in part 809.

(15) An Application for an Investigational Device Exemption, described in part 812.

(16) Data and information about a medical device submitted as part of the procedures for classifying these devices, described in section 513.

(17) Data and information about a medical device submitted as part of the procedures for establishing, amending, or repealing a standard for these devices, described in section 514.

(18) An application for premarket approval of a medical device, described in section 515.

(19) A product development protocol for a medical device, described in section 515.

(20) Data and information about an electronic product submitted as part of the procedures for establishing, amending, or repealing a standard for these products, described in section 358 of the Public Health Service Act.

(21) Data and information about an electronic product submitted as part of the procedures for obtaining a variance from any

electronic product performance standard, as described in 1010.4.

(22) Data and information about an electronic product submitted as part of the procedures for granting, amending, or extending an exemption from a radiation safety performance standard, as described in 1010.5.

(23) Data and information about a clinical study of an infant formula when submitted as part of an infant formula notification under section 412(c) of the Federal Food, Drug, and Cosmetic Act.

(24) Data and information submitted in a petition for a nutrient content claim, described in 101.69 of this chapter, or for a health claim, described in 101.70 of this chapter.

(25) Data and information from investigations involving children submitted in a new dietary ingredient notification, described in 190.6 of this chapter.

Application for research or marketing permit includes: [21 CFR § 56]

(1) A color additive petition, described in part 71.

(2) Data and information regarding a substance submitted as part of the procedures for establishing that a substance is generally recognized as safe for a use which results or may reasonably be expected to result, directly or indirectly, in its becoming a component or otherwise affecting the characteristics of any food, described in 170.35.

(3) A food additive petition, described in part 171.

(4) Data and information regarding a food additive submitted as part of the procedures regarding food additives permitted to be used on an interim basis pending additional study, described in 180.1.

(5) Data and information regarding a substance submitted as part of the procedures for establishing a tolerance for unavoidable contaminants in food and food-packaging materials, described in section 406 of the act.

(6) An investigational new drug application, described in part 312 of this chapter.

(7) A new drug application, described in part 314.

(8) Data and information regarding the bioavailability or bioequivalence of drugs for human use submitted as part of the procedures for issuing, amending, or repealing a bioequivalence requirement, described in part 320.

(9) Data and information regarding an over-the-counter drug for human use submitted as part of the procedures for classifying such drugs as generally recognized as safe and effective and not misbranded, described in part 330.

(10) An application for a biologics license, described in part 601 of this chapter.

(11) Data and information regarding a biological product submitted as part of the procedures for determining that licensed biological products are safe and effective and not misbranded, as described in part 601 of this chapter.

(12) An Application for an Investigational Device Exemption, described in part 812.

(13) Data and information regarding a medical device for human use submitted as part of the procedures for classifying such devices, described in part 860.

(14) Data and information regarding a medical device for human use submitted as part of the procedures for establishing, amending, or repealing a standard for such device, described in part 861.

(15) An application for premarket approval of a medical device for human use, described in section 515 of the act.

(16) A product development protocol for a medical device for human use, described in section 515 of the act.

(17) Data and information regarding an electronic product submitted as part of the procedures for establishing, amending, or repealing a standard for such products, described in section 358 of the Public Health Service Act.

(18) Data and information regarding an electronic product submitted as part of the procedures for obtaining a variance from any electronic product performance standard, as described in 1010.4.

(19) Data and information regarding an electronic product submitted as part of the procedures for granting, amending, or extending an exemption from a radiation safety performance standard, as described in 1010.5.

(20) Data and information regarding an electronic product submitted as part of the procedures for obtaining an exemption from notification of a radiation safety defect or failure of compliance with a radiation safety performance standard, described in subpart D of part 1003.

(21) Data and information about a clinical study of an infant formula when submitted as part of an infant formula notification under section 412(c) of the Federal Food, Drug, and Cosmetic Act.

(22) Data and information submitted in a petition for a nutrient content claim, described in 101.69 of this chapter, and for a health claim, described in 101.70 of this chapter.

(23) Data and information from investigations involving children submitted in a new dietary ingredient notification, described in 190.6 of this chapter.

Application for research or marketing permit includes: [21 CFR § 58]

(1) A color additive petition, described in part 71.

(2) A food additive petition, described in parts 171 and 571.

(3) Data and information regarding a substance submitted as part of the procedures for establishing that a substance is generally recognized as safe for use, which use results or may reasonably be expected to result, directly or indirectly, in its becoming a component or otherwise affecting the characteristics of any food, described in 170.35 and 570.35.

(4) Data and information regarding a food additive submitted as part of the procedures regarding food additives permitted to be used on an interim basis pending additional study, described in 180.1.

(5) Aninvestigational new drug application, described in part 312 of this chapter.

(6) Anew drug application, described in part 314.

(7) Data and information regarding an over-the-counter drug for human use, submitted as part of the procedures for classifying such drugs as generally recognized as safe and effective and not misbranded, described in part 330.

(8) Data and information about a substance submitted as part of the procedures for establishing a tolerance for unavoidable contaminants in food and food-packaging materials, described in parts 109 and 509.

(9) [Reserved]

(10) A Notice of Claimed Investigational Exemption for a New Animal Drug, described in part 511.

(11) A new animal drug application, described in part 514.

(12) [Reserved]

(13) An application for a biologics license, described in part 601 of this chapter.

(14) An application for an investigational device exemption, described in part 812.

(15) An Application for Premarket Approval of a Medical Device, described in section 515 of the act.

(16) A Product Development Protocol for a Medical Device, described in section 515 of the act.

(17) Data and information regarding a medical device submitted as part of the procedures for classifying such devices, described in part 860.

(18) Data and information regarding a medical device submitted as part of the procedures for establishing, amending, or repealing a performance standard for such devices, described in part 861.

(19) Data and information regarding an electronic product submitted as part of the procedures for obtaining an exemption from notification of a radiation safety defect or failure of compliance with a radiation safety performance standard, described in subpart D of part 1003.

(20) Data and information regarding an electronic product submitted as part of the procedures for establishing, amending, or repealing a standard for such product, described in section 358 of the Public Health Service Act.

(21) Data and information regarding an electronic product submitted as part of the procedures for obtaining a variance from any electronic product performance standard as described in 1010.4.

(22) Data and information regarding an electronic product submitted as part of the procedures for granting, amending, or extending an exemption from any electronic product performance standard, as described in 1010.5.

(23) A premarket notification for a food contact substance, described in part 170, subpart D, of this chapter.

Approval letter means a written communication to an applicant from FDA approving an application or an abbreviated application. [21 CFR § 314]

Assent means a child's affirmative agreement to participate in a clinical investigation. Mere failure to object may not, absent affirmative agreement, be construed as assent. [21 CFR § 50]

Assess the effects of the change means to evaluate the effects of a manufacturing change on the identity, strength, quality, purity, and potency of a drug product as these factors may relate to the safety or effectiveness of the drug product. [21 CFR § 314]

Authorized generic drug means a listed drug, as defined in this section, that has been approved under section 505(c) of the act and is marketed, sold, or distributed directly or indirectly to retail class of trade with labeling, packaging (other than repackaging as the listed drug in blister packs, unit doses, or similar packaging for use in institutions), product code, labeler code, trade name, or trademark that differs from that of the listed drug. [21 CFR § 314]

B

Batch means a specific quantity or lot of a test or control article that has been characterized according to 58.105(a). [21 CFR § 58]

Batch means a specific quantity of a drug or other material that is intended to have uniform character and quality, within specified limits, and is produced according to a single manufacturing order during the same cycle of manufacture. [21 CFR § 210]

Bioavailability means the rate and extent to which the active ingredient or active moiety is absorbed from a drug product and becomes available at the site of action. For drug products that are not intended to be absorbed into the bloodstream, bioavailability may be assessed by measurements intended to reflect the rate and extent to which the active ingredient or active moiety becomes available at the site of action. [21 CFR § 320]

Bioequivalence means the absence of a significant difference in the rate and extent to which the active ingredient or active moiety in pharmaceutical equivalents or pharmaceutical alternatives becomes available at the site of drug action when administered at the same molar dose under similar conditions in an appropriately designed study. Where there is an intentional difference in rate (e.g., in certain extended release dosage forms), certain pharmaceutical equivalents or alternatives may be considered bioequivalent if there is no significant difference in the extent to which the active ingredient or moiety from each product becomes available at the site of drug action. This applies only if the difference in the rate at which the active ingredient or moiety becomes available at the site of drug action is intentional and is reflected in the proposed labeling, is not essential to the attainment of effective body drug concentrations on chronic use, and is considered medically insignificant for the drug. [21 CFR § 320]

Bioequivalence requirement means a requirement imposed by the Food and Drug Administration for in vitro and/or in vivo testing of specified drug products which must be satisfied as a condition of marketing. [21 CFR § 320]

Biometrics means a method of verifying an individual's identity based on measurement of the individual's physical feature(s) or repeatable action(s) where those features and/or actions are both unique to that individual and measurable. [21 CFR § 11]

C

Children means persons who have not attained the legal age for consent to treatments or procedures involved in clinical investigations, under the applicable law of the jurisdiction in which the clinical investigation will be conducted. [21 CFR § 50]

Class 1 resubmission means the resubmission of an application or efficacy supplement, following receipt of a complete response letter, that contains one or more of the following: Final printed labeling, draft labeling, certain safety updates, stability updates to support provisional or final dating periods, commitments to perform postmarketing studies (including proposals for such studies), assay validation data, final release testing on the last lots used to support approval, minor reanalyses of previously submitted data, and other comparatively minor information. [21 CFR § 314]

Class 2 resubmission means the resubmission of an application or efficacy supplement, following receipt of a complete response letter, that includes any item not specified in the definition of "Class 1 resubmission," including any item that would require presentation to an advisory committee. [21 CFR § 314]

Closed system means an environment in which system access is controlled by persons who are responsible for the content of electronic records that are on the system. [21 CFR § 11]

Clinical investigation means any experiment that involves a test article and one or more human subjects and that either is subject to requirements for prior submission to the Food and Drug Administration under section 505(i) or 520(g) of the act, or is not subject to requirements for prior submission to the Food and Drug Administration under these sections of the act, but the results of which are intended to be submitted later to, or held for inspection by, the Food and Drug Administration as part of an application for a research or marketing permit. The term does not include experiments that are subject to the provisions of part 58 of this chapter, regarding nonclinical laboratory studies. [21 CFR § 50]

Clinical investigation means any experiment that involves a test article and one or more human subjects, and that either must meet the requirements for prior submission to the Food and Drug Administration under section 505(i) or 520(g) of the act, or need not meet the requirements for prior submission to the Food and Drug Administration under these sections of the act, but the results of which are intended to be later submitted to, or held for inspection by, the Food and Drug Administration as part of an application for a research or marketing permit. The term does not include experiments that must meet the provisions of part 58, regarding nonclinical laboratory studies. The termsresearch, clinical research, clinical study, study, andclinical investigation are deemed to be synonymous for purposes of this part. [21 CFR § 56]

Clinical investigation means any experiment in which a drug is administered or dispensed to, or used involving, one or more human subjects. For the purposes of this part, an experiment is any use of a drug except for the use of a marketed drug in the course of medical practice. [21 CFR § 312]

Clinical investigator means only a listed or identified investigator or subinvestigator who is directly involved in the treatment or evaluation of research subjects. The term also includes the spouse and each dependent child of the investigator. [21 CFR § 54]

Compensation affected by the outcome of clinical studies means compensation that could be higher for a favorable outcome than for an unfavorable outcome, such as compensation that is explicitly greater for a favorable result or compensation to the investigator in the form of an equity interest in the sponsor of a covered study or in the form of compensation tied to sales of the product, such as a royalty interest. [21 CFR § 54]

Complete response letter means a written communication to an applicant from FDA usually describing all of the deficiencies that the agency has identified in an application or abbreviated application that must be satisfactorily addressed before it can be approved. [21 CFR § 314]

Component means any ingredient intended for use in the manufacture of a drug product, including those that may not appear in such drug product. [21 CFR § 210]

Contract research organization means a person that assumes, as an independent contractor with the sponsor, one or more of the obligations of a sponsor, e.g., design of a protocol, selection or monitoring of investigations, evaluation of reports, and preparation of materials to be submitted to the Food and Drug Administration. [21 CFR § 312]

Control article means any food additive, color additive, drug, biological product, electronic product, medical device for human use, or any article other than a test article, feed, or water that is administered to the test system in the course of a nonclinical laboratory study for the purpose of establishing a basis for comparison with the test article. [21 CFR § 58]

Covered clinical study means any study of a drug or device in humans submitted in a marketing application or reclassification petition subject to this part that the applicant or FDA relies on to establish that the product is effective (including studies that show equivalence to an effective product) or any study in which a single investigator makes a significant contribution to the demonstration of safety. This would, in general, not include phase 1 tolerance studies or pharmacokinetic studies, most clinical pharmacology studies (unless they are critical to an efficacy determination), large open safety studies conducted at multiple sites, treatment protocols, and parallel track protocols. An applicant may consult with FDA as to which clinical studies constitute "covered clinical studies" for purposes of complying with financial disclosure requirements. [21 CFR § 54]

Custom device means a device that: [21 CFR § 812]

(1) Necessarily deviates from devices generally available or from an applicable performance standard or premarket approval requirement in order to comply with the order of an individual physician or dentist;

(2) Is not generally available to, or generally used by, other physicians or dentists;

(3) Is not generally available in finished form for purchase or for dispensing upon prescription;

(4) Is not offered for commercial distribution through labeling or advertising; and

(5) Is intended for use by an individual patient named in the order of a physician or dentist, and is to be made in a specific form for that patient, or is intended to meet the special needs of the physician or dentist in the course of professional practice.

D

Digital signature means an electronic signature based upon cryptographic methods of originator authentication, computed by using a set of rules and a set of parameters such that the identity of the signer and the integrity of the data can be verified. [21 CFR § 11]

Drug product means a finished dosage form, for example, tablet, capsule, solution, etc., that contains an active drug ingredient generally, but not necessarily, in association with inactive ingredients. The term also includes a finished dosage form that does not contain an active ingredient but is intended to be used as a placebo. [21 CFR § 210]

> *Drug product* means a finished dosage form, for example, tablet, capsule, or solution, that contains a drug substance, generally, but not necessarily, in association with one or more other ingredients. [21 CFR § 314]

> *Drug product* means a finished dosage form, e.g., tablet, capsule, or solution, that contains the active drug ingredient, generally, but not necessarily, in association with inactive ingredients. [21 CFR § 320]

Drug substance means an active ingredient that is intended to furnish pharmacological activity or other direct effect in the diagnosis, cure, mitigation, treatment, or prevention of disease or to affect the structure or any function of the human body, but does not include intermediates use in the synthesis of such ingredient. [21 CFR § 314]

E, F

Efficacy supplement means a supplement to an approved application proposing to make one or more related changes from among the following changes to product labeling: [21 CFR § 314]

(1) Add or modify an indication or claim;

(2) Revise the dose or dose regimen;

(3) Provide for a new route of administration;

(4) Make a comparative efficacy claim naming another drug product;

(5) Significantly alter the intended patient population;

(6) Change the marketing status from prescription to over-the-counter use;

(7) Provide for, or provide evidence of effectiveness necessary for, the traditional approval of a product originally approved under subpart H of part 314; or

(8) Incorporate other information based on at least one adequate and well-controlled clinical study.

Electronic record means any combination of text, graphics, data, audio, pictorial, or other information representation in digital form that is created, modified, maintained, archived, retrieved, or distributed by a computer system. [21 CFR § 11]

Electronic signature means a computer data compilation of any symbol or series of symbols executed, adopted, or authorized by an individual to be the legally binding equivalent of the individual's handwritten signature. [21 CFR § 11]

Emergency use means the use of a test article on a human subject in a life-threatening situation in which no standard acceptable treatment is available, and in which there is not sufficient time to obtain IRB approval. [21 CFR § 56]

Family member means any one of the following legally competent persons: Spouse; parents; children (including adopted children); brothers, sisters, and spouses of brothers and sisters; and any individual related by blood or affinity whose close association with the subject is the equivalent of a family relationship. [21 CFR § 50]

FDA means the Food and Drug Administration. [21 CFR § 312, § 314, § 812, § 814]

Fiber means any particulate contaminant with a length at least three times greater than its width. [21 CFR § 210]

G, H

Gang-printed labeling means labeling derived from a sheet of material on which more than one item of labeling is printed. [21 CFR § 210]

Guardian means an individual who is authorized under applicable State or local law to consent on behalf of a child to general medical care when general medical care includes participation in research. For purposes of subpart D of this part, a guardian also means an individual who is authorized to consent on behalf of a child to participate in research. [21 CFR § 50]

Handwritten signature means the scripted name or legal mark of an individual handwritten by that individual and executed or adopted with the present intention to authenticate a writing in a permanent form. The act of signing with a writing or marking instrument such as a pen or stylus is preserved. The scripted name or legal mark, while conventionally applied to paper, may also be applied to other devices that capture the name or mark. [21 CFR § 11]

HDE means a premarket approval application submitted pursuant to this subpart seeking a humanitarian device exemption from the effectiveness requirements of sections 514 and 515 of the act as authorized by section 520(m)(2) of the act. [21 CFR § 814]

HUD (humanitarian use device) means a medical device intended to benefit patients in the treatment or diagnosis of a disease or condition that affects or is manifested in fewer than 4,000 individuals in the United States per year. [21 CFR § 814]

Human subject means an individual who is or becomes a participant in research, either as a recipient of the test article or as a control. A subject may be either a healthy human or a patient. [21 CFR § 50]

Human subject means an individual who is or becomes a participant in research, either as a recipient of the test article or as a control. A subject may be either a healthy individual or a patient. [21 CFR § 56]

IDE means an approved or considered approved investigational device exemption under section 520(g) of the act and parts 812 and 813. [21 CFR § 814]

Implant means a device that is placed into a surgically or naturally formed cavity of the human body if it is intended to remain there for a period of 30 days or more. FDA may, in order to protect public health, determine that devices placed in subjects for shorter periods are also "implants" for purposes of this part. [21 CFR § 812]

Inactive ingredient means any component other than anactive ingredient. [21 CFR § 210]

Increased frequency of adverse drug experience is an increased rate of occurrence of a particular serious adverse drug event, expected or unexpected, after appropriate adjustment for drug exposure. [21 CFR § 514]

IND means an investigational new drug application. For purposes of this part, "IND" is synonymous with "Notice of Claimed Investigational Exemption for a New Drug." [21 CFR § 312]

Independent ethics committee (IEC) means a review panel that is responsible for ensuring the protection of the rights, safety, and well-being of human subjects involved in a clinical investigation and is adequately constituted to provide assurance of that protection. An institutional review board (IRB), as defined in 56.102(g) of this chapter and subject to the requirements of part 56 of this chapter, is one type of IEC. [21 CFR § 312]

In-process material means any material fabricated, compounded, blended, or derived by chemical reaction that is produced for, and used in, the preparation of the drug product.

Institution means any public or private entity or agency (including Federal, State, and other agencies). The wordfacility as used in section 520(g) of the act is deemed to be synonymous with the terminstitution for purposes of this part. [21 CFR § 50, § 56]

Institution means a person, other than an individual, who engages in the conduct of research on subjects or in the delivery of medical services to individuals as a primary activity or as an adjunct to providing residential or custodial care to humans. The term includes, for example, a hospital, retirement home, confinement facility, academic establishment, and device manufacturer. The term has the same meaning as "facility" in section 520(g) of the act. [21 CFR § 812]

Institutional review board (IRB) means any board, committee, or other group formally designated by an institution to review biomedical research involving humans as subjects, to approve the initiation of and conduct periodic review of such research. The term has the same meaning as the phraseinstitutional review committee as used in section 520(g) of the act. [21 CFR § 50]

> *Institutional Review Board (IRB)* means any board, committee, or other group formally designated by an institution to review, to approve the initiation of, and to conduct periodic review of, biomedical research involving human subjects. The primary purpose of such review is to assure the protection of the rights and welfare of the human subjects. The term has the same meaning as the phraseinstitutional review committee as used in section 520(g) of the act. [21 CFR § 56]

> *Institutional review board (IRB)* means any board, committee, or other group formally designated by an institution to review biomedical research involving subjects and established, operated, and functioning in conformance with part 56. The term has the same meaning as "institutional review committee" in section 520(g) of the act. [21 CFR § 812]

Investigation means a clinical investigation or research involving one or more subjects to determine the safety or effectiveness of a device. [21 CFR § 812]

Investigational device means a device, including a transitional device, that is the object of an investigation. [21 CFR § 812]

Investigational new drug means a new drug or biological drug that is used in a clinical investigation. The term also includes a biological product that is used in vitro for diagnostic purposes. The terms "investigational drug" and "investigational new drug" are deemed to be synonymous for purposes of this part. [21 CFR § 312]

Investigator means an individual who actually conducts a clinical investigation, i.e., under whose immediate direction the test article is administered or dispensed to, or used involving, a subject, or, in the event of an investigation conducted by a team of individuals, is the responsible leader of that team. [21 CFR § 50, § 56]

> ***Investigator*** means an individual who actually conducts a clinical investigation (i.e. , under whose immediate direction the drug is administered or dispensed to a subject). In the event an investigation is conducted by a team of individuals, the investigator is the responsible leader of the team. "Subinvestigator" includes any other individual member of that team. [21 CFR § 312]

> ***Investigator*** means an individual who actually conducts a clinical investigation, i.e., under whose immediate direction the test article is administered or dispensed to, or used involving, a subject, or, in the event of an investigation conducted by a team of individuals, is the responsible leader of that team. [21 CFR § 812]

IRB approval means the determination of the IRB that the clinical investigation has been reviewed and may be conducted at an institution within the constraints set forth by the IRB and by other institutional and Federal requirements. [21 CFR § 56]

J, K, L

Legally authorized representative means an individual or judicial or other body authorized under applicable law to consent on behalf of a prospective subject to the subject's particpation in the procedure(s) involved in the research. [21 CFR § 50]

Listed drug means a new drug product that has an effective approval under section 505(c) of the act for safety and effectiveness or under section 505(j) of the act, which has not been withdrawn or suspended under section 505(e)(1) through (e)(5) or (j)(5) of the act, and which has not been withdrawn from sale for what FDA has determined are reasons of safety or effectiveness. Listed drug status is evidenced by the drug product's identification as a drug with an effective approval in the current edition of FDA's "Approved Drug Products with Therapeutic Equivalence Evaluations" (the list) or any current supplement thereto, as a drug with an effective approval. A drug product is deemed to be a listed drug on the date of effective approval of the application or abbreviated application for that drug product. [21 CFR § 314]

Lot means a batch, or a specific identified portion of a batch, having uniform character and quality within specified limits; or, in the case of a drug product produced by continuous process, it is a specific identified amount produced in a unit of time or quantity in a manner that assures its having uniform character and quality within specified limits. [21 CFR § 210]

Lot number, control number, or batch number means any distinctive combination of letters, numbers, or symbols, or any combination of them, from which the complete history of the manufacture, processing, packing, holding, and distribution of a batch or lot of drug product or other material can be determined. [21 CFR § 210]

M

Manufacture, processing, packing, or holding of a drug product includes packaging and labeling operations, testing, and quality control of drug products. [21 CFR § 210]

Marketing application means an application for a new drug submitted under section 505(b) of the act or a biologics license application for a biological product submitted under the Public Health Service Act. [21 CFR § 312]

Master file means a reference source that a person submits to FDA. A master file may contain detailed information on a specific manufacturing facility, process, methodology, or component used in the manufacture, processing, or packaging of a medical device. [21 CFR § 814]

Medicated feed means any Type B or Type C medicated feed as defined in 558.3 of this chapter. The feed contains one or more drugs as defined in section 201(g) of the act. The manufacture of medicated feeds is subject to the requirements of part 225 of this chapter. [21 CFR § 210]

Medicated premix means a Type A medicated article as defined in 558.3 of this chapter. The article contains one or more drugs as defined in section 201(g) of the act. The manufacture of medicated premixes is subject to the requirements of part 226 of this chapter. [21 CFR § 210]

Minimal risk means that the probability and magnitude of harm or discomfort anticipated in the research are not greater in and of themselves than those ordinarily encountered in daily life or during the performance of routine physical or psychological examinations or tests. [21 CFR § 50, § 56]

Monitor, when used as a noun, means an individual designated by a sponsor or contract research organization to oversee the progress of an investigation. The monitor may be an employee of a sponsor or a consultant to the sponsor, or an employee of or consultant to a contract research organization.Monitor, when used as a verb, means to oversee an investigation. [21 CFR § 812]

N

NADA is a new animal drug application including all amendments and supplements. [21 CFR § 514]

Newly acquired information means data, analyses, or other information not previously submitted to the agency, which may include (but are not limited to) data derived from new clinical studies, reports of adverse events, or new analyses of previously submitted data (e.g., meta-analyses) if the studies, events or analyses reveal risks of a different type or greater severity or frequency than previously included in submissions to FDA. [21 CFR § 314, § 814]

Nonapplicant is any person other than the applicant whose name appears on the label and who is engaged in manufacturing, packing, distribution, or labeling of the product. [21 CFR § 514]

Nonclinical laboratory study means in vivo or in vitro experiments in which test articles are studied prospectively in test systems under laboratory conditions to determine their safety. The term

---

does not include studies utilizing human subjects or clinical studies or field trials in animals. The term does not include basic exploratory studies carried out to determine whether a test article has any potential utility or to determine physical or chemical characteristics of a test article. [21 CFR § 58]

Nonfiber releasing filter means any filter, which after appropriate pretreatment such as washing or flushing, will not release fibers into the component or drug product that is being filtered. [21 CFR § 210]

Noninvasive, when applied to a diagnostic device or procedure, means one that does not by design or intention: (1) Penetrate or pierce the skin or mucous membranes of the body, the ocular cavity, or the urethra, or (2) enter the ear beyond the external auditory canal, the nose beyond the nares, the mouth beyond the pharynx, the anal canal beyond the rectum, or the vagina beyond the cervical os. For purposes of this part, blood sampling that involves simple venipuncture is considered noninvasive, and the use of surplus samples of body fluids or tissues that are left over from samples taken for noninvestigational purposes is also considered noninvasive. [21 CFR § 812]

O, P

Open system means an environment in which system access is not controlled by persons who are responsible for the content of electronic records that are on the system. [21 CFR § 11]

Original application means a pending application for which FDA has never issued a complete response letter or approval letter, or an application that was submitted again after FDA had refused to file it or after it was withdrawn without being approved. [21 CFR § 314]

Parent means a child's biological or adoptive parent. [21 CFR § 50]

Percentage of theoretical yield means the ratio of the actual yield (at any appropriate phase of manufacture, processing, or packing of a particular drug product) to the theoretical yield (at the same phase), stated as a percentage. [21 CFR § 210]

Permission means the agreement of parent(s) or guardian to the participation of their child or ward in a clinical investigation. Permission must be obtained in compliance with subpart B of this part and must include the elements of informed consent described in 50.25. [21 CFR § 50]

Person includes an individual, partnership, corporation, association, scientific or academic establishment, government agency, or organizational unit thereof, and any other legal entity. [21 CFR § 58]

> *Person* includes any individual, partnership, corporation, association, scientific or academic establishment, Government agency or organizational unit of a Government agency, and any other legal entity. [21 CFR § 812]

> *Person* includes any individual, partnership, corporation, association, scientific or academic establishment, Government agency, or organizational unit thereof, or any other legal entity. [21 CFR § 814]

Pharmaceutical alternatives means drug products that contain the identical therapeutic moiety, or its precursor, but not necessarily in the same amount or dosage form or as the same salt or ester. Each such drug product individually meets either the identical or its own respective compendial or other applicable standard of identity, strength, quality, and purity, including potency and, where applicable, content uniformity, disintegration times and/or dissolution rates. [21 CFR § 320]

Pharmaceutical equivalents means drug products in identical dosage forms that contain identical amounts of the identical active drug ingredient,i.e. , the same salt or ester of the same therapeutic moiety, or, in the case of modified release dosage forms that require a reservoir or overage or such forms as prefilled syringes where residual volume may vary, that deliver identical amounts of the active drug ingredient over the identical dosing period; do not necessarily contain the same inactive ingredients; and meet the identical compendial or other applicable standard of identity, strength, quality, and purity, including potency and, where applicable, content uniformity, disintegration times, and/or dissolution rates. [21 CFR § 320]

PMA means any premarket approval application for a class III medical device, including all information submitted with or incorporated by reference therein. "PMA" includes a new drug application for a device under section 520(1) of the act. [21 CFR § 814]

PMA amendment means information an applicant submits to FDA to modify a pending PMA or a pending PMA supplement. [21 CFR § 814]

PMA supplement means a supplemental application to an approved PMA for approval of a change or modification in a class III medical device, including all information submitted with or incorporated by reference therein. [21 CFR § 814]

> *30-day PMA supplement* means a supplemental application to an approved PMA in accordance with 814.39(e). [21 CFR § 814]

Potential applicant means any person: [21 CFR § 514]

(1) Intending to investigate a new animal drug under section 512(j) of the Federal Food, Drug, and Cosmetic Act (the act),

(2) Investigating a new animal drug under section 512(j) of the act,

(3) Intending to file a new animal drug application (NADA) or supplemental NADA under section 512(b)(1) of the act, or

(4) Intending to file an abbreviated new animal drug application (ANADA) under section 512(b)(2) of the act.

Presubmission conference means one or more conferences between a potential applicant and FDA to reach a binding agreement establishing a submission or investigational requirement. [21 CFR § 514]

Presubmission conference agreement means that section of the memorandum of conference headed "Presubmission Conference Agreement" that records any agreement on the submission or investigational requirement reached by a potential applicant and FDA during the presubmission conference. [21 CFR § 514]

Product defect/manufacturing defect is the deviation of a distributed product from the standards specified in the approved application, or any significant chemical, physical, or other change, or deterioration in the distributed drug product, including any microbial or chemical contamination. A manufacturing defect is a product defect caused or aggravated by a manufacturing or related process. A manufacturing defect may occur from a single event or from deficiencies inherent to the manufacturing process. These defects are generally associated with product contamination, product deterioration, manufacturing error, defective packaging, damage from disaster, or labeling error. For example, a labeling error may include any incident that causes a distributed product to be mistaken for, or its labeling applied to, another product. [21 CFR § 514]

Proprietary interest in the tested product means property or other financial interest in the product including, but not limited to, a patent, trademark, copyright or licensing agreement. [21 CFR § 54]

Q, R

Quality assurance unit means any person or organizational element, except the study director, designated by testing facility management to perform the duties relating to quality assurance of nonclinical laboratory studies. [21 CFR § 58]

Quality control unit means any person or organizational element designated by the firm to be responsible for the duties relating to quality control. [21 CFR § 210]

Raw data means any laboratory worksheets, records, memoranda, notes, or exact copies thereof, that are the result of original observations and activities of a nonclinical laboratory study and are necessary for the reconstruction and evaluation of the report of that study. In the event that exact transcripts of raw data have been prepared (e.g., tapes which have been transcribed verbatim, dated, and verified accurate by signature), the exact copy or exact transcript may be substituted for the original source as raw data.Raw data may include photographs, microfilm or microfiche copies, computer printouts, magnetic media, including dictated observations, and recorded data from automated instruments. [21 CFR § 58]

Reasonable probability means that it is more likely than not that an event will occur. [21 CFR § 814]

Reference listed drug means the listed drug identified by FDA as the drug product upon which an applicant relies in seeking approval of its abbreviated application. [21 CFR § 314]

Representative sample means a sample that consists of a number of units that are drawn based on rational criteria such as random sampling and intended to assure that the sample accurately portrays the material being sampled. [21 CFR § 210]

Resubmission means submission by the applicant of all materials needed to fully address all deficiencies identified in the complete response letter. An application or abbreviated application for which FDA issued a complete response letter, but which was withdrawn before approval and later submitted again, is not a resubmission. [21 CFR § 314]

Right of reference or use means the authority to rely upon, and otherwise use, an investigation for the purpose of obtaining approval of an application, including the ability to make available the underlying raw data from the investigation for FDA audit, if necessary. [21 CFR § 314]

S

Same drug product formulation means the formulation of the drug product submitted for approval and any formulations that have minor differences in composition or method of manufacture from the formulation submitted for approval, but are similar enough to be relevant to the agency's determination of bioequivalence. [21 CFR § 320]

Serious adverse drug experience is an adverse event that is fatal, or life-threatening, or requires professional intervention, or causes an abortion, or stillbirth, or infertility, or congenital anomaly, or prolonged or permanent disability, or disfigurement. [21 CFR § 514]

Serious, adverse health consequences means any significant adverse experience, including those which may be either life-threatening or involve permanent or long term injuries, but excluding injuries that are nonlife-threatening and that are temporary and reasonably reversible. [21 CFR § 814]

Significant equity interest in the sponsor of a covered study
means any ownership interest, stock options, or other financial
interest whose value cannot be readily determined through
reference to public prices (generally, interests in a nonpublicly
traded corporation), or any equity interest in a publicly traded
corporation that exceeds $50,000 during the time the clinical
investigator is carrying out the study and for 1 year following
completion of the study. [21 CFR § 54]

Significant payments of other sorts means payments made by the
sponsor of a covered study to the investigator or the institution to
support activities of the investigator that have a monetary value of
more than $25,000, exclusive of the costs of conducting the
clinical study or other clinical studies, (e.g., a grant to fund
ongoing research, compensation in the form of equipment or
retainers for ongoing consultation or honoraria) during the time
the clinical investigator is carrying out the study and for 1 year
following the completion of the study. [21 CFR § 54]

Significant risk device means an investigational device that: [21 CFR
§ 812]

(1) Is intended as an implant and presents a potential for serious
risk to the health, safety, or welfare of a subject;

(2) Is purported or represented to be for a use in supporting or
sustaining human life and presents a potential for serious risk
to the health, safety, or welfare of a subject;

(3) Is for a use of substantial importance in diagnosing, curing,
mitigating, or treating disease, or otherwise preventing
impairment of human health and presents a potential for
serious risk to the health, safety, or welfare of a subject; or

(4) Otherwise presents a potential for serious risk to the health,
safety, or welfare of a subject.

Specification means the quality standard (i.e. , tests, analytical
procedures, and acceptance criteria) provided in an approved
application to confirm the quality of drug substances, drug
products, intermediates, raw materials, reagents, components, in-
process materials, container closure systems, and other materials
used in the production of a drug substance or drug product. For
the purpose of this definition,acceptance criteria means numerical
limits, ranges, or other criteria for the tests described. [21 CFR §
314]

Specimen means any material derived from a test system for examination or analysis. [21 CFR § 58]

Sponsor means a person who initiates a clinical investigation, but who does not actually conduct the investigation, i.e., the test article is administered or dispensed to or used involving, a subject under the immediate direction of another individual. A person other than an individual (e.g., corporation or agency) that uses one or more of its own employees to conduct a clinical investigation it has initiated is considered to be a sponsor (not a sponsor-investigator), and the employees are considered to be investigators. [21 CFR § 50]

> *Sponsor* means a person or other entity that initiates a clinical investigation, but that does not actually conduct the investigation, i.e., the test article is administered or dispensed to, or used involving, a subject under the immediate direction of another individual. A person other than an individual (e.g., a corporation or agency) that uses one or more of its own employees to conduct an investigation that it has initiated is considered to be a sponsor (not a sponsor-investigator), and the employees are considered to be investigators. [21 CFR § 56]

Sponsor means: [21 CFR § 58]

> (1) A person who initiates and supports, by provision of financial or other resources, a nonclinical laboratory study;
>
> (2) A person who submits a nonclinical study to the Food and Drug Administration in support of an application for a research or marketing permit; or
>
> (3) A testing facility, if it both initiates and actually conducts the study.

Sponsor means a person who takes responsibility for and initiates a clinical investigation. The sponsor may be an individual or pharmaceutical company, governmental agency, academic institution, private organization, or other organization. The sponsor does not actually conduct the investigation unless the sponsor is a sponsor-investigator. A person other than an individual that uses one or more of its own employees to conduct an investigation that it has initiated is a sponsor, not a sponsor-investigator, and the employees are investigators. [21 CFR § 312]

Sponsor means a person who initiates, but who does not actually conduct, the investigation, that is, the investigational device is administered, dispensed, or used under the immediate direction of another individual. A person other than an individual that uses one or more of its own employees to conduct an investigation that it has initiated is a sponsor, not a sponsor-investigator, and the employees are investigators. [21 CFR § 812]

Sponsor of the covered clinical study means the party supporting a particular study at the time it was carried out. [21 CFR § 54]

Sponsor-investigator means an individual who both initiates and actually conducts, alone or with others, a clinical investigation, i.e., under whose immediate direction the test article is administered or dispensed to, or used involving, a subject. The term does not include any person other than an individual, e.g., corporation or agency. [21 CFR § 50]

Sponsor-investigator means an individual who both initiates and actually conducts, alone or with others, a clinical investigation, i.e., under whose immediate direction the test article is administered or dispensed to, or used involving, a subject. The term does not include any person other than an individual, e.g., it does not include a corporation or agency. The obligations of a sponsor-investigator under this part include both those of a sponsor and those of an investigator. [21 CFR § 56]

Sponsor-Investigator means an individual who both initiates and conducts an investigation, and under whose immediate direction the investigational drug is administered or dispensed. The term does not include any person other than an individual. The requirements applicable to a sponsor-investigator under this part include both those applicable to an investigator and a sponsor. [21 CFR § 312]

Sponsor-investigator means an individual who both initiates and actually conducts, alone or with others, an investigation, that is, under whose immediate direction the investigational device is administered, dispensed, or used. The term does not include any person other than an individual. The obligations of a sponsor-investigator under this part include those of an investigator and those of a sponsor. [21 CFR § 812]

Statement of material fact means a representation that tends to show that the safety or effectiveness of a device is more probable than it would be in the absence of such a representation. A false affirmation or silence or an omission that would lead a reasonable person to draw a particular conclusion as to the safety or effectiveness of a device also may be a false statement of material fact, even if the statement was not intended by the person making it to be misleading or to have any probative effect. [21 CFR § 814]

Strength means: [21 CFR § 210]

(i) The concentration of the drug substance (for example, weight/weight, weight/volume, or unit dose/volume basis), and/or

(ii) The potency, that is, the therapeutic activity of the drug product as indicated by appropriate laboratory tests or by adequately developed and controlled clinical data (expressed, for example, in terms of units by reference to a standard).

Study completion date means the date the final report is signed by the study director. [21 CFR § 58]

Study director means the individual responsible for the overall conduct of a nonclinical laboratory study. [21 CFR § 58]

Study initiation date means the date the protocol is signed by the study director. [21 CFR § 58]

Subject means a human who participates in an investigation, either as a recipient of the investigational new drug or as a control. A subject may be a healthy human or a patient with a disease. [21 CFR § 312]

Subject means a human who participates in an investigation, either as an individual on whom or on whose specimen an investigational device is used or as a control. A subject may be in normal health or may have a medical condition or disease. [21 CFR § 812]

T

Termination means a discontinuance, by sponsor or by withdrawal of IRB or FDA approval, of an investigation before completion. [21 CFR § 812]

Test article means any drug (including a biological product for human use), medical device for human use, human food additive, color additive, electronic product, or any other article subject to regulation under the act or under sections 351 and 354-360F of the Public Health Service Act (42 U.S.C. 262 and 263b-263n). [21 CFR § 50]

> **Test article** means any drug for human use, biological product for human use, medical device for human use, human food additive, color additive, electronic product, or any other article subject to regulation under the act or under sections 351 or 354-360F of the Public Health Service Act. [21 CFR § 56]

> **Test article** means any food additive, color additive, drug, biological product, electronic product, medical device for human use, or any other article subject to regulation under the act or under sections 351 and 354-360F of the Public Health Service Act. [21 CFR § 58]

Test system means any animal, plant, microorganism, or subparts thereof to which the test or control article is administered or added for study. Test system also includes appropriate groups or components of the system not treated with the test or control articles. [21 CFR § 58]

Testing facility means a person who actually conducts a nonclinical laboratory study, i.e., actually uses the test article in a test system. Testing facility includes any establishment required to register under section 510 of the act that conducts nonclinical laboratory studies and any consulting laboratory described in section 704 of the act that conducts such studies. Testing facility encompasses only those operational units that are being or have been used to conduct nonclinical laboratory studies. [21 CFR § 58]

The list means the list of drug products with effective approvals published in the current edition of FDA's publication "Approved

Drug Products with Therapeutic Equivalence Evaluations" and any current supplement to the publication. [21 CFR § 314]

Theoretical yield means the quantity that would be produced at any appropriate phase of manufacture, processing, or packing of a particular drug product, based upon the quantity of components to be used, in the absence of any loss or error in actual production. [21 CFR § 210]

Transitional device means a device subject to section 520(l) of the act, that is, a device that FDA considered to be a new drug or an antibiotic drug before May 28, 1976. [21 CFR § 812]

U, V

Unanticipated adverse device effect means any serious adverse effect on health or safety or any life-threatening problem or death caused by, or associated with, a device, if that effect, problem, or death was not previously identified in nature, severity, or degree of incidence in the investigational plan or application (including a supplementary plan or application), or any other unanticipated serious problem associated with a device that relates to the rights, safety, or welfare of subjects. [21 CFR § 812]

Unexpected adverse drug experience is an adverse event that is not listed in the current labeling for the new animal drug and includes any event that may be symptomatically and pathophysiologically related to an event listed on the labeling, but differs from the event because of greater severity or specificity. For example, under this definition hepatic necrosis would be unexpected if the labeling referred only to elevated hepatic enzymes or hepatitis. [21 CFR § 514]

W, X, Y, Z

Ward means a child who is placed in the legal custody of the State or other agency, institution, or entity, consistent with applicable Federal, State, or local law. [21 CFR § 50]

Index

About the author

Mindy J. Allport-Settle was born in Beckley and raised in Oak Hill, West Virginia. She moved to North Carolina to attend the N.C. School of the Arts for high school and now lives near Raleigh. Following in the footsteps of Gordon Allport, all of her books are built on a foundation of psychology and sociology with a focus on improving some aspect of industry through research and education.

Her career in healthcare began when she was a teenager working as an emergency medical technician. Since then, she has joined the U.S. Navy's advanced hospital corps, worked in organ and human tissue procurement, specialized in ophthalmology, and moved on to serve as a key executive, board member, and consultant for some of the best companies in the pharmaceutical, medical device, and biotechnology industry. She has provided guidance in regulatory compliance, corporate structuring, restructuring and turnarounds, new drug submissions, research and development and product commercialization strategies, and new business development. Her experience and dedication have resulted in international recognition as the developer of the only FDA-recognized and benchmarked quality systems training and development business methodology.

Her education includes a Bachelor's degree from the University of North Carolina, an MBA in Global Management from the University of Phoenix, and completion of the corporate governance course series in audit committees, compensation committees, and board effectiveness at Harvard Business School.

About PharmaLogika

Since 2002, PharmaLogika, Inc has established itself as one of the world's premier consulting firms for Pharmaceutical, Biotech, and Medical Device companies across the globe. In so doing, it has earned the trust of executives in Life Sciences for its integrity, accuracy, and unwavering commitment to independent thought with regard to its products and services as well as those of its customers. Through www.PharmaLogika.com, its involvement in sponsored events, and personal references it has reached millions in print and online. Its mission, to provide flawlessly designed and executed products and services to startups as well as established industry leaders to facilitate their growth from discovery and clinical trial navigation to the commercialization and marketing of their products.

PharmaLogika consults with pharmaceutical, biotech, and medical device quality units to provide third party audits, training, pre approval inspections (PAIs), compliance remediation, and a portfolio of related quality and regulatory affairs products and services. Those products include but are not limited to Quality Assurance Forms, SOP and clinical templates, and the highly successful Integrated Development Training System.

Regulatory action guidance as well as quality systems guidance are delivered as part of its standard products and services. Through the use of highly skilled resources throughout the process, each offering is designed to enact a comprehensive quality systems approach in addressing Quality Assurance (QA) issues. The results insure a close adherence to current Good Manufacturing Practice (cGMP) standards.

PharmaLogika also has a Research and Development OTC line for human consumption that targets alpha 1-antitrypsin deficiency, Fibromyalgia, Restless Legs Syndrome, and Attention Deficit Disorder. A veterinary OTC is currently available that provides canine and feline oral debriding and cleansing agents as well as a stain remover and topical antiseptic. These products combine to provide a strong pipeline of both current and future deliverables.

Other books available

Current Good Manufacturing Practices: Pharmaceutical, Biologics, and Medical Device Regulations and Guidance Documents Concise Reference

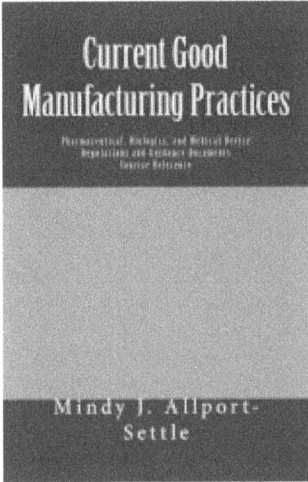

Good Manufacturing Practice (GMP) Guidelines: The Rules Governing Medicinal Products in the Eurpean Union, EudraLex Volume 4 Concise Reference

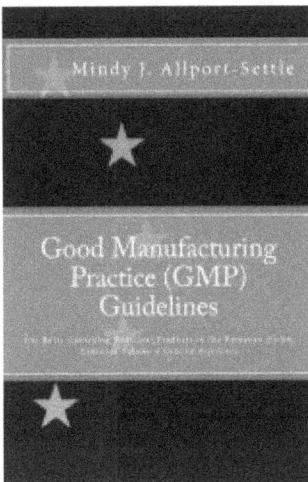

International Conference on Harmonisation (ICH) Quality Guidelines: Pharmaceutical, Biologics, and Medical Device Guidance Documents Concise Reference

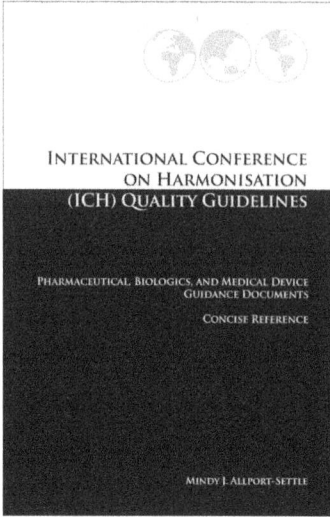

FDA Acronyms, Abbreviations and Terminology: Human and Veterinary Regualtory Reference

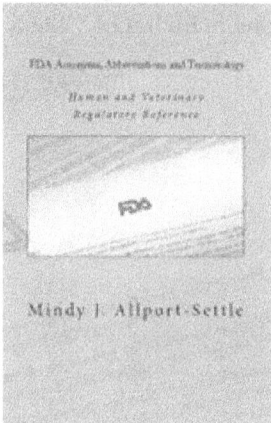

Course Development 101: Developing Training Programs for Regulated Industries

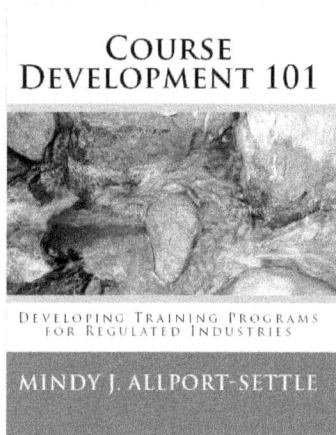

Compliance Remediation for Pharmaceutical Manufacturing: A Project Management Guide for Re-establishing FDA Compliance

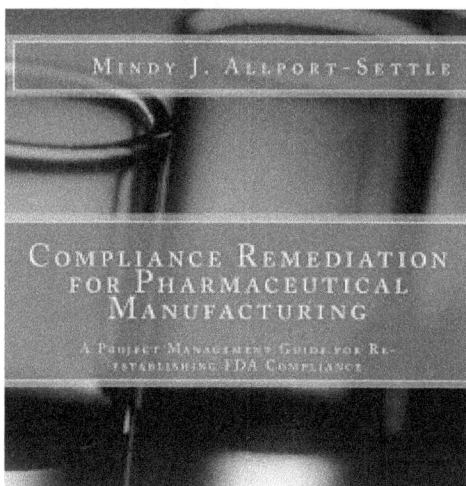

Investigations Operations Manual: FDA Field Inspection and
Investigation Policy and Procedure Concise Reference

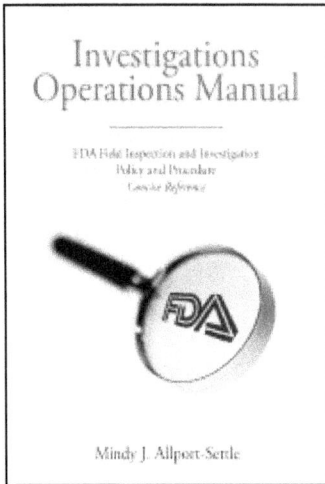

FDA Establishment Inspections: Pharmaceutical, Biotechnology, Medical
Device and Food Manufacturing Concise Reference

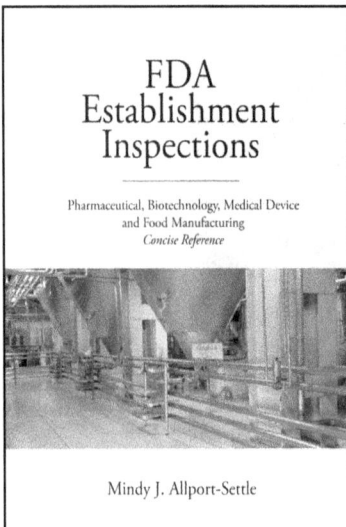

Canadian Good Manufacturing Practices: Pharmaceutical, Biotechnology, and Medical Device Regulations and Guidance Concise Reference

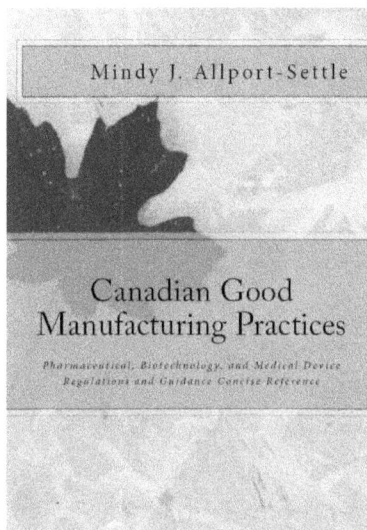

Good Clinical Practice: Pharmaceutical, Biologics, and Medical Device Regulations and Guidance Documents Concise Reference; Volume 1, Regulations and Volume 2, Guidance

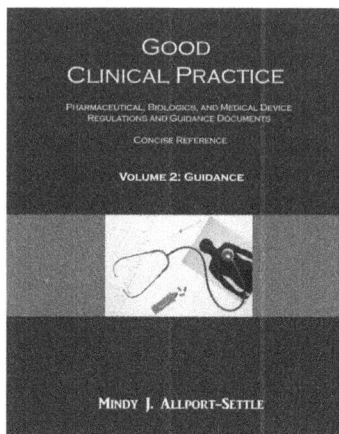

Please visit www.PharmaLogika.com for additional titles and for a list of resellers

or visit your favorite local or internet book seller.